Assassin's Mace

A Chinese Game Changer

杀手锏

Assassin's Mace
A Chinese Game Changer

Brigadier Saif Ul Islam Khan

(Established 1870)

United Service Institution of India
New Delhi

Vij Books India Pvt Ltd
New Delhi (India)

Published by

Vij Books India Pvt Ltd
(Publishers, Distributors & Importers)
2/19, Ansari Road
Delhi – 110 002
Phones: 91-11-43596460, 91-11-47340674
Fax: 91-11-47340674
e-mail: vijbooks@rediffmail.com

Copyright © 2015, United Service Institution of India, New Delhi

ISBN (Pb)   : 9789385563034 (2016)

All rights reserved.

No part of this book may be reproduced, stored in a retrieval system, transmitted or utilised in any form or by any means, electronic, mechanical, photocopying, recording or otherwise, without the prior permission of the copyright owner. Application for such permission should be addressed to the publisher.

The views expressed in the book are of the author and not necessarily those of the USI or publishers.

Dedicated to my parents……

Dr Mohammad Islamullah Khan, MBBS, MS, DO
and
Mrs Zubaida Islam Khan

Contents

Foreword	ix
Preface	xi
Acknowledgement	xv
List of Abbreviations	xvii

Chapters

I	China's Strategic Concerns	1
II	Evolution of the Assassin's Mace	18
III	Shashoujian in War Fighting Strategies	25
IV	Trends in Chinese Assassin's Mace	40
V	Countering The Dragon	72

Tables	88
Index	99

List of Tables

1	US Forces In Japan	88
2	US Forces In Republic of Korea	90
3	US Forces In Pacific Ocean and Australia	92
4	China And India (1949-2001): Use Of Force And War	93
5	Sino-India Armed Forces Comparison	94
6	Sino-India Armed Forces Structure Comparison	95
7	Sino-India Navy Comparison	96
8	Sino-India Air Force Comparison	97

List of Illustrations

1	US Forces In Asia Pacific	13
2	EMP burst over India	46

Foreword

The book, 'Assassin's Mace – A Chinese Game Changer' provides invaluable concepts into the asymmetric warfare strategies, which the People's Liberation Army has enmeshed into its current operational philosophy and military strategic thinking. This book also provides a unique insight into the strategic time lines in which Assassin's Mace can be used.

China's military traditions are derived from historical and cultural backgrounds which are very different from rest of the world. Strategies, guile, deception and methods to secure an upper hand over the adversary are inherent in Chinese military culture. To the rest of the world, asymmetric warfare may be a format to be included in planning, for the Chinese it is but a natural process. The Assassin's Mace weapons or 'Shashoujian' as Chinese call them, are asymmetric warfare weapons of today. From the name it appears that concept focuses on developing one weapon capable of creating a master stroke, in reality it is the evolution of systems of weapon to be used at different stages of battle. The thought behind use of these weapons is to have a crippling effect on the enemy's operational plans.

This book analyses China's security concerns and issues that drive its military modernisation process and also the war fighting strategies which facilitate use of Assassin's Mace. The author tries to integrate Assassin's Mace weapons in 'Key point strikes' and 'active defence' strategies that China propagates.

China sees itself as a 'Great Power in Asia' and considers India as its major regional competitor. Both the countries have been developing their military forces incorporating high technology weapons in their modernization plans. The author tries to analyze the relationship between these two nuclear weapon nations and brings out the implication of 'Chinese Assassin's Mace' program on India.

'Assassin's Mace – A Chinese Game Changer' is an essential resource for those who seek to understand the trajectory of People's Liberation Army's transformation and is an indispensable compendium for every researcher who wants to study 'PLA Military Strategy' in a holistic manner.

March 2015

Lt Gen P.K. Singh,
PVSM, AVSM (Retd)
Director, United Service Institution of India

Preface

My research on Chinese Military Modernisation took me to China where I was able to interact with the People's Liberation Army officials and academicians. While I noticed a distinct pride in them towards the trajectory of Chinese military modernisation, there seemed an underlying fear of US and its capacity to contain China with help of its allies. A foreboding that India could jump on to the US bandwagon for strategic gains played high on their minds. While accepting that US was way ahead in the field of military technology, they found solace in some strengths they have. They spoke of informationalisation and active defence but with a chant similar to the content of White Papers on Defence issued from Beijing. They appeared confident that the US will not train its guns on them. The seed of their confidence apparently lay in the 'Assassin's Mace Weapons' program which the country is developing with earnest.

This book, which focuses on the evolution of Assassin's Mace program and its likely future trajectory, is intended as a resource for strategic analysts and students seeking to understand the nuances relating to Assassin's Mace and the trends of high technology warfare in future conflicts. The book addresses the concept of employment of Assassin's Mace Weapons as a deterrence tool for conflicts and as a magic wand for achieving victory in war. Assassin's Mace weapons transcend the realms of strategic deception, surprise, military guile, technological wonder and intelligent warfare strategies and make them powerful combat disruption tools. As I tread into the domains of strategist, academician and a technocrat during the discourse in the book, my endeavour has been to be lucid and refrain from use of jargon. To facilitate the understanding of the not-so-common concepts and terminologies, I have taken help of notes.

The framework of the book includes a broad analysis of China's Security concerns, the internal and external security threats that manifest today, and impinge on China's National Interests. The analysis, done with

Chinese perspective in mind, takes us to China's perception of being 'boxed in' and contained by superior US forces, in conjunction with countries in the periphery. From this derives the scenario of conflict, a danger which could roll back the China growth story. The book thus initially focuses on security concerns that could impinge on China's National interests and then proceeds to bring out the necessity for China to modernize its military and develop Assassin's Mace.

A conflict with its toughest adversary, the US, could seriously affect China's growth trajectory. Roll back from a journey that is leading to attainment of numero uno status in the world is unacceptable to China. Wisdom of her military strategist advice - deter war. China has thus sought to develop asymmetric capabilities in warfare to deter a conflict with US. The focus of the second Chapter is on evolution of combat disruptive technologies by China. In my discourse with analysts, I noticed certain grey areas in the comprehension of Chinese modernisation of military and concept of Assassin's Mace weapons development program. I have endeavoured to shed light on these grey zones, and bring to fore the concept of Assassin's Mace, its salient features and employment philosophy; and thereby delineate it from a standard military modernisation program.

For the development of Assassin's Mace weapons there is a need for a meaningful technological and industrial base. If China was to invest large sums of money in Assassin's Mace Weaponry, the focus needed to be correct. Chinese strategists analysed wars that US had been engaged in the recent past to focus their work on building an understanding of the US strengths and vulnerabilities so that the strategies to counter US could be arrived at.

Amongst the various wars analysed by the Chinese, the Kosovo Campaign, in which foreign military intervention took place to resolve country's 'internal issues' was of importance to China as she has three potential hot spots, Tibet, Xinjiang and Taiwan, which could trigger foreign intervention. This kind of military intervention in Tibet, Xinjiang or Taiwan would challenge the Chinese Core Interest - its territorial integrity. The Falkland wars taught important lessons for People's Liberation Army (Navy) and People's Liberation Army (Air Force). The Iran-Iraq war brought in lessons on employment of missiles, while the revolution in military affairs and the dazzle of the wars in Gulf sent the Chinese back to the drawing board. From the drawing board, came out the modernisation plan, a de-novo concept of operations; and hinged to it the Assassin's Mace development program. The third Chapter addresses the integration of Assassin's Mace weapons in war-fighting strategies. To facilitate understanding, the Chapter initially brings out broad concept of operations of Assassin's Mace time phased strikes; there-after a detailed analyses of the strategy. The deliberations draw out strategies which China is likely to employ/ would employ in case of conflict with the US without going into the wars per se. Integration of Shashoujian in 'War Fighting Strategies' has been discussed in time phased employment of the Assassin's Mace. I would suggest to those who wish to develop greater understanding of People's Liberation Army and its transformation to read the lessons that China has learnt from other people's wars.

The fourth chapter, looks at the trends in development of Assassin's Mace Weaponry. I have refrained from breaking this longish chapter for sake of continuity of thought. Each trend in Assassin's Mace weaponry, to the extent possible, has been explained with either technological growth time line or a historical perspective, the aim being two folds - firstly, to facilitate understanding of technology and secondly, to use historical data as the basis to develop understanding of the trend. Additional information has been added to give an inkling of how things are likely to progress in future. Assassin's Mace transcends the boundaries of military operations and technological development which I have endeavoured to bridge by explanatory insertions at appropriate places.

While US is China's global threat, India is China's regional competition. The unresolved border dispute and growing number of divergences make Sino-China conflict a possibility. The last chapter covers the broad canvas of military modernisation being undertaken by both countries and focuses on security implications for India. An attempt has been made to bring out deficiencies in India's security apparatus and possible options to resolve them. Certain recommendations as a 'way ahead' for India have also been included. Issues relating to doctrinal changes, higher defence organisations, logistics and infrastructural trends have not been addressed to maintain the orientation towards the Assassin's Mace and its influence on a future Sino-India conflict.

Acknowledgement

This book though authored by me is a result of experiences and research of many individuals and institutions. At the foremost is the United Services Institution of India which has not only served as a harbinger and facilitator to my research but also provided me an environment full of very capable, knowledgeable and extremely helpful analysts on global affairs and strategic issues.

First, I would like to thank my guide, Major General BK Sharma, AVSM, SM & Bar, who brought focus to my study on combat disruptive technologies being developed by China and guided me onto this fascinating world of Chinese Assassin's Mace program. I learnt a lot from his advice and guidance on the subject as well as on related strategic issues.

I express my heartfelt thanks to Major General YS Gera, the head of the research team at United Services Institution of India, who encouraged me to share by research work in the form of a book.

I would also like to express gratitude to my colleagues at the United Services Institution of India for sharing their experiences and giving constructive criticism, which were of immense benefit to me in writing the book. The support of Colonel NSP Bisht, who worked with me on Chinese Military Modernisation, was invaluable. His understanding of global affairs and ability to gauge 'unstated' implications of world events greatly assisted me in understanding the larger picture. Colonel Sanjeev Relia's knowledge on Cyber Warfare and related issues helped me to develop a better understanding of what China calls 'informationalisation'. Discourses on nuclear issues with Dr Roshan Khaniejo and discussions on strategic affairs with Colonel Vishal Murada were extremely useful. I thank them for sharing their wisdom with me.

I have also benefitted greatly from discussions over the years with my fellow 'men in olive-greens' as also the sea going 'men in white', who formed part of my professional life over last twenty seven years in the Indian Armed Forces.

I am in debt to, my wife, Gul, who supported me throughout the project and proof read all my drafts and scripts painstakingly. My son, Saad and my daughter, Sameera, assisted me not only in proof reading but also in keying in the script, when my fingers needed a rest. This book and my research would not have happened had it not been for my mother, Zubaida Islam Khan, my sisters, Yasmin, Farah and Nasreen, who at the end of my father's burial, showed unbelievable strength to take on the grief alone, and forced me to leave for time critical research assignment on the subject.

I would like to thank Lieutenant General PK Singh, PVSM, AVSM Director, United Services Institution of India, Member, IISS, London, Governing Council Member, Indian Council of World Affairs, New Delhi and a former Army Commander of the Indian Army, who not only read and appreciated my book but also for adding value and substance to my book by writing such a meaningful foreword.

- Brigadier Saif Ul Islam Khan

List of Abbreviations

ABS	Air Based Shashoujian
ADIZ	Air Defence Identification Zone
AEW&C	Airborne Early Warning And Control
AF	Air Force
AMCA	Advanced Multirole Combat Aircraft
ASBM	Anti-Ship ballistic missile
ASAT	Anti-Satellite
ASCM	Anti-Ship Cruise missile
ASEAN	Association of Southeast Asian Nations
AWACS	Airborne Warning and Control System
CAR	Central Asian Republics
CASIC	China Aerospace Science and Industry Corporation
CBG	Carrier Battle Groups
CCP	Chinese Communist Party
C4ISR	Command, Control, Communications, Computers, Intelligence, Surveillance and Reconnaissance
CNO	Computer Network Operations
COG	Centers of Gravity
COSTIND	Commissions of Science, Technology and Industry for National Defence

CSIS	Centre for Strategic and International Studies
DEW	Directed Energy Weapon
DRDO	Defence Research and Development Organization
EMP	Electro Magnetic Pulse
EW	Electronic Warfare
FAE	Fuel Air Explosives
GDP	Gross Domestic Product
GPS	Global Positioning System
HEMP	High-altitude Electromagnetic Pulse
HPM	High Power Microwave
ICBM	Intercontinental Ballistic Missile
IOR	Indian Ocean Region
IRBM	Intermediate Range Ballistic Missile
ISR	Intelligence, Surveillance, Reconnaissance
IW	Information Warfare
KKV	Kinetic Kill Vehicle
KMT	Kuomintang
LAC	Line of Actual Control
LACM	Land Attack Cruise Missiles
LBS	Land Based Shashoujian
LEO	Low Earth Orbit
LCAC	Landing Craft Air Cushion
LHA	Landing Helicopter Assault
LPD	Landing Platform Dock

Abbreviations

MaRVs	Maneuverable Re-entry Vehicles
MEMS	Micro Electro Mechanical Systems
MIRV	Multiple Independently Targetable Re-entry Vehicle
MRBM	Medium Range Ballistic Missile
NEMP	Nuclear Electromagnetic Pulse
NNEMP	Non-Nuclear Electromagnetic Pulse
OSS	Oceanic Strike Shashoujian
OTH	Over The Horizon
PGM	Precision Guided Munition
PLA	People's Liberation Army
PLAAF	People's Liberation Army Air Force
PLAN	People's Liberation Army Navy
PLD	Portable Laser Distributor
PRC	People's Republic of China
RF	Radio Frequency
RMA	Revolution in Military Affairs
RPG	Rocket Propelled Grenade
RRF	Rapid Reaction Forces
SAM	Surface-to-Air Missile
SBS	Space Based Shashoujian
SLOCs	Sea Lines of Communication
SOF	Special Operation Forces
SRBM	Short-Range Ballistic Missile
SSBN	Ship Submersible Ballistic missile Nuclear

SSM	Surface to Surface Missile
TAR	Tibetan Autonomous Region
THAAD	Terminal High Altitude Area Defence
UAV	Unmanned Aerial Vehicle
UCAV	Unmanned Combat Aerial Vehicle
UCP	Unmanned Combat Platform
UHF	Ultra High frequency
USAF	United States Air Force
UUCV	Unmanned Underwater Combat Vehicles
UUV	Unmanned Underwater Vehicles

China's Strategic Concerns

"We should draw on the experiences in new military changes of the world and seize the opportunities to achieve leapfrog development in national defence and army modernisation."

— **Hu Jintao**

Four years after the culmination of the Second World War, China's struggles continued as she fought to liberate herself of all foreign intrusions and end the civil war that raged across the country. As independent China took birth as People's Republic of China (PRC) in 1949, Mao Zedong said, *"Chinese people have stood up. They will never again be humiliated"*.[1] The "hundred years" of suffering and humiliation China had met at the hands of foreign powers had dented National pride. China rose to avenge herself with heart filled with anger and hurt nationalism. The architects of new China focussed on strengthening agriculture, economy and industrial development. They also made plans to systematically modernise and transform the Chinese Military - the People's Liberation Army (PLA).

There was an apparent lack of understanding of China across the world at that time. Implications of Mao Zedong's words were not taken too seriously. Engrossed in their own national dynamics and global play, countries failed to correctly assess China's potential to reconfigure herself and metamorphose from a weak nation to one that could affect the global order. China's phenomenal rise in a broad array of activities took the world by surprise. In a relatively short span of time, her economic prowess enabled China to not only transform her socio-economic landscape but also affect the contours of global politico-economic relationships and geo-strategic alignments.

The astonishing growth curve that won the respect of nations, by some aggressive actions by China, resulted in inducing a 'Chinese fear factor' in regional and global spheres. A perception was born that an assertive China was on the path of a regional hegemon and had great global ambitions. She was considered to have scant regard for others while in pursuit of her National interests, this despite PRC's effort to hard sell its rise as 'peaceful and harmonious '. The impact of China's rise and the 'Chinese fear factor' across the globe can be assessed from a global survey conducted by Centre for Strategic and International Studies (CSIS) in February 2009 which indicate that 38 per cent considered China the biggest threat in today's world, North Korea, the second greatest threat (21 per cent) while the United States of America (US), with 12.9 per cent, took the third place.[2]

US ability to influence global affairs was a source of grave concern to China. China was certain that the old political and economical order, which they felt was unfair and uncertain, had to be changed fundamentally. The Chinese analysts questioned the world systems stating that economic development of the world was unequal that the developing countries gained lesser from global proceeds. They argued that democracy in international relations remained elusive and economic progress was unbalanced and disadvantageous to China. While security problems were still unresolved new issues appeared on the arena. They feared that US and her allies followed a policy that sought to 'contain' China. China decided to unremittingly put the new security concept into practice, oppose all kinds of hegemonism and power politics.[3]

China's view came to the fore in the China's National Defence, White Paper, 2004 where it has been assessed that the "military factor" plays a greater role in international configuration and national security and that "the forms of war are undergoing changes from mechanization to informationalization". It has been stated that the confrontation between systems has become "the principal feature of confrontation" on the battlefield.

The wisdom of Sun Tzu, respected for centuries by the Chinese, articulates on need to work on defeating an enemy's plan, rather than his forces. Chinese analysed the operational concepts of their toughest likely adversary, the US. They analysed the recent wars undertaken by the US and her allies, and arrived at a strategy to counter US hegemonic designs. In its strategy, the Chinese indicate a realistic approach and have avoided the temptation to attempt to be strong in every facet of war fighting. A focus on complete force modernisation and development of the Armed Forces in all spheres would deplete the finances and material resources. Hence, China took a considered decision to develop specific strengths aimed at targeting specific US weaknesses. They evaluated the strengths and weaknesses of the US military and evolved a plan to develop asymmetric capacities to address the US military vulnerabilities. Asymmetry can be created by delineation of enemy's weaknesses from the strengths and developing appropriate resources to counter it. When successfully applied, asymmetric warfare can deny the opponent the initiative which he seeks to obtain, create a psychological impact that reduces the effectiveness of the decision makers and the military forces while at the same time enables the user to retain the operational and strategic initiative.

Historically, China has experience in use of asymmetry in war. Practice of asymmetry in war is enshrined in the Chinese strategic thoughts in Sun Tzu's "Art of War" and in "36 Stratagems". However, in the current century, the moot questions that need answers are:-

(a) What is the need for asymmetry in war in the present era, especially when Chinese military modernisation is well on track?

(b) What threatens China that compels it to invest huge sums of money into military ware, which it could otherwise use gainfully in National development?

The answer lies in China's growth story and its future ambitions. China as an emerging Great Power, and sees the Western Pacific, South Asia and Indian Ocean Region (IOR), as its natural sphere of influence. China's concerns lie in the fact that US plays a major role in the region, and is not in favour of the emergence of a regional power that treads onto the space US currently enjoys. In the South Asian and IOR, India is emerging and has significant influence. US, Japan and Indian interests are bound to conflict with those of China. A conflict with China's National interests can cause instability in the region. China needed a trump card, a magic wand, a powerful tool by which it can deter hostile designs of other stake holders. China needs it's 'Assassin's Mace' to have a psychological ascendancy over regional countries and US. She needed the Assassin's Mace to protect her National interest till she attains stature of a major global player. Thus, analysis of China's National interests and security concerns is essential to get a correct perspective of China's desire to develop asymmetric warfare capability.

China's National Interests

National interests govern the National policies and strategies are the way ahead that a nation seeks for itself. National interests help to appreciate the behavioural characteristics of a country, its actions and reactions to situations and the manner in which its development program take shape. It is correct to assume that for a Nation its core interests are stable, but these are not necessarily unchallengeable or immutable. Yan Xuetong defined national interest as 'the common material and spiritual' need of all the people of a nation state. He indicated that a nation needs 'security and development' and 'respect and recognition' from the international community. China's national interest comprises of three main ingredients, viz. development interests, sovereignty interests and responsibility interests.[4] Ka Po Ng argues that although China is a multi-national state the concept of national interests is used as a unified nation state and the concept is built on the appeal to nationalism. He considers the most fundamental national interest for China is the preservation of its sovereignty and pursuit of sovereignty related interests.[5]

Since Deng Xiaoping considered national interest as the basis of all government policies and he placed economic development as the core national interest. Deng Xiaoping's three step agenda for the pursuit of China's national interests was for maintenance of peace, realization of unification and increase in the pace of economic construct.[6] Two out of the three issues are sovereignty related, hence the sovereignty matters are rated high and of serious concern for China.

At the US-China Strategic Economic Dialogue in July 2009, Chinese State Councillor Dai Bingguo mentioned China's "Core National Interests" as safe guarding Chinese fundamental systems and national security, maintaining national sovereignty and territorial integrity, and ensuring sustained and stable development of China's economy and society.[7] The Councillor thus placed on record that maintenance of the Chinese Communist Party's (CCP) control over China, ensuring control on its internal ethnic and other domestic discords (including democracy movement)and preventing external aggressive designs, the "one China" policy and economic development as the Core interests for China. As China progressed economically, its consumption of energy and natural resources increased, its trade expanded necessitating open sea lanes and secure off shore bases. The need for maritime security and maritime interests became an integral part of China's security considerations. The instability in internal security issues and the external environment can affect national interests and can cause a nation to go into turmoil and even disintegrate, if it fails to restore itself to a stable state. Can an Assassin's Mace program help in safe guarding National interests ? Do the dynamics of external security environment and internal security environment undergo a change if China possesses Assassin's Mace Weapons ? Relevant internal and external security issues affecting China and their effect on evolution of Assassin's Mace program need a careful study.

Internal Security Issues

China has a number of internal issues that drive her strategic discourse. China is bordered by rugged terrain from virtually all directions enclosing her core area which in the yesteryears was the natural defence obstacle from the invaders. Today, the geographical disposition of resources and the uneven population distribution can be a destabilizing factor for China. Her internal issues arise out of her geography, population, demographic distribution, age profile, inequitable economic distribution, demands for democracy, growth of religious fundamentalism and so on. East-West divide amongst the Chinese populace is pronounced due to differential economic prosperity and ethno-religious disparities. Any economic slowdown poses internal security threats for China. The socio-economic divide between the 'haves' and 'have-nots' could reflect as sharper social strife, increase in crime rates etc. The possibility of this triggering larger nation-wide unrest is real and hence remains a major security concern for China. Trend of ageing population threatens to deprive China of the required work force, essential for continued economic growth. This age imbalance will raise the Chinese State's economic burden on social security and healthcare for the burgeoning old and unproductive population. Hence, to prevent internal issues - China has to grow economically.

The CCP was founded on a Marxist philosophy and proletariat role in the society. As China shifts towards socialist form of Capitalism, CCP uses nationalism and economic development as tools to maintain its control over China. The Party ensures this by repeatedly reminding the citizens of the historical rivalries and of the '100 years of humiliation'[8] and further incorporating its members at all levels of society including the rank and file of PLA. To keep the Party's position maintained, the spirit of

'Nationalism' has to be sustained.

Economic development has been the bedrock of social stability and could disrupt and cause domestic instability. Economic development is of concern to China. As per projections by Chinese Government, the first quarter of 2014 saw a growth rate of 7.7%. However, others estimate a much lower rate of economic growth. The double digits economic growth rates for China is the story of the past.[9] Economic downturn would rank high on the Party's list of nightmares as failure to grow will not only challenge the authority of the Party but would give scope to some to spring up issues related to internal domestic frictions.

Failure to attain national objectives would directly undermine the CCP's credibility as the sole political entity capable of looking after the nation's interest. It is of vital interest to the Party and thus to the State, that China must achieve stated national objective even if this leads to war. Thus for China, Tibetan strife for independence, Dalai Lama influence in the Tibetan Autonomous Region (TAR) and beyond China's boundaries, extremists' movement and influence of Taliban on its western borders are of concern. To offset the demographic imbalance China has facilitated shifting of Han population in these areas and is developing large scale infrastructure and undertaken militarization of the western buffer region. China resorts to ruthless suppression of any movement for independence or democracy but possibility of the US and India sponsored unrest in these areas threatens China.

Assassin's Mace program provides for a cost effective solution for security. China can progress development of Assassin's Mace at much lesser cost, save precious finances to grow further and modernize its entire Armed Forces based on timelines. Growing nation with developing military will help to keep the citizen's faith in CCP.

External Security Issues

China's unshakable national commitment' has been stressed in the White Paper on 'The Diversified Employment of China's Armed Forces 2013', and it has been brought out that China opposes any form of 'hegemonism or power politics,' and 'does not interfere in the internal affairs of other countries'. It has been emphasised that 'China will never seek hegemony or behave in a hegemonic manner, nor will it engage in military expansion'.[10] Having stated this in its opening sentences, the White Paper goes to explain plethora of military developments with rationale that hints otherwise. Analysis of China's relationship with its neighbours and the US as also certain actions taken over the years and discussed later indicate a difference in words uttered and actual unfolding of events.

The Chinese leadership identified the first quarter of 21st Century (up to 2025) as a period of 'Strategic Opportunity' and the next (2025-2050) for 'Strategic Expansion' and for securing her National Goal of becoming a **'Great Power'**. The relationship with its neighbours and other global players in the region will have an impact on China's attainment of its status of a Great Power.

> 'A Great Power 'is a state that is recognized as having the ability to exert its influence on a global scale. Great powers characteristically possess military and economic strength, as well as diplomatic and soft power influence, which may cause small powers to consider the great powers' opinions before taking actions of their own. International relations theorists have posited that great power status can be characterized into power capabilities, spatial aspects and status dimensions.
>
> Source: Wikipedia

Sino-Japan Relationship

Japan and China have been historical rivals, rivalries dating back to the 19th century. According to the Chinese Government, some 'sensitive issues' between Japan and the PRC are issues 'relating to history', the issues of Taiwan, as integral part of China, issue of Diaoyu Islands, 'issue of war reparations', 'Japanese chemical weapons discarded in China' and 'issue of Guanghualiao' remains.[11] The later part of 2013 saw tensions escalating to new high over issues of Air Defence Identification Zone (ADIZ) over Diaoyu/Senkaku Islands. Japan considers that China is 'expected to recognize its responsibility as a major power, accept and stick to the international norms and play a more active and cooperative role in regional and global issues'. Japan has expressed concerns that China has been engaging in extensive, rapid modernization of its military forces, backed by continual substantial increases in its defence budget. Japanese white paper 2013 has stressed that the growth of China's military power must be accompanied by greater clarity of its strategic intentions in order to avoid causing friction in the region.[12] Japanese Prime Minister Abe's visit to war shrines and establishment of an ADIZ over Diaoyu/Senkaku Islands by the Chinese, rhetoric by media of both countries has heightened tensions in the area. US reactions to these incidents brought in the question of US as a reliable ally to the forefront. For China, Japan poses a threat to its regional dominance. Further the US – Japan relation, the likely US-Japan–India cooperation, the Australia angle to Asia problem are significant concerns. A weak and secluded Japan favours China. Assassin's Mace program has significant deterrence value and also has the capability of keeping US away from regional configuration. If China succeeds in achieving this, it would make a significant impact in the functioning of tomorrow's world order.

Korean Peninsula

China considers that stability of Korean peninsula is vital for the peace and stability of the entire East Asian region and China sponsored Six Party Talks to prevent conflict from breaking out in the Korean peninsula. China fears instability in the Korean peninsula would provide the US with an excuse to expand its military presence around China's maritime borders. Her inability to control North Korean can lessen China's credibility and status as regional power. Power struggles in the Korean peninsula or a military conflict in the region can set back China's timelines of attaining the status of great power.

Taiwan

China considers Taiwan an integral part of China and that the Taiwan issue is therefore a "domestic issue". The "One China" principle is the underlying premise and foundation for discussions between China and Taiwan. Hu Jintao's farewell remarks and Xi Jinping's opening remarks as President stressed on the Taiwan reunification as their primary security concern, and that China will not hesitate to go to war to achieve it. Despite occasional rhetoric, China's has been following an (unstated) policy for the graduated integration of Taiwan into mainland China. The Economic Cooperation Framework Agreement of 2010 gave a boost to commerce and trade between Taiwan and China, and caters for approximately 40 percent of Taiwanese exports. Large numbers of Taiwanese companies continue to invest in 'Mainland China'; tourism is bridging people to people contact. The KMT regime of Taiwan appears to be heading towards an informal 'One Country Two Systems.' However, some Taiwanese feel enhancement in trade and tourism is better for mainland China's democratic re-orientation.[13] The US arms transfers to Taiwan and the centrality of the Taiwan question in the US Asia calculus is a threat to China and she holds the US responsible for the arms transfers and hegemonic intents; and for interference in its 'domestic affairs'. Inability to make Taiwan part of the governing authority in mainland China would be considered a major failure by her citizens. Hence, for next few decades keeping US away from Taiwan would be considered victory by the Chinese. Assassin's Mace weapons development may help achieve this.

South East Asian Region

South East Asia's importance as a traffic link between the Pacific and Indian Oceans, through the Straits of Malacca and the South China Sea, is undeniable. The countries in South East Asia have endeavoured to achieve political stability and ensure steady economic growth through ASEAN and other forums as well as bilateral negotiations. This region's destabilizing factors include the territorial dispute over the South China Sea, ethnic minority issues, piracy and extremist groups. However, China's assertiveness, specifically related to the South China Sea islands dispute, has induced the "China fear factor". Like the Korean Peninsula, instability in the South China Sea provides an excuse to the US and Japan to extend their military footprint in China's immediate neighbourhood which China is keen to avoid. Indian collaborations in the field of oil and gas in South China Sea is an unwelcome development for China. China considers South China Sea as extremely important in case of contest with the US or other regional powers.[14] The US declaration, in ASEAN Regional Forum meeting at Hanoi (in 2010), that it has a 'national interest' in the continued freedom of navigation in the region[15] has added to the instability in the region. The bilateral disputes that China has with some member states (Vietnam, Philippines, Brunei and Indonesia) have the potential to strain and stall relations with ASEAN as a whole.[16]

Weaponisation of South East Asian region has been significant and new military alliances have taken shape. US - Indonesia concluded a comprehensive partnership package and the Indonesia military modernization package includes 24 F-16 fighters from the US, four

C-130 transport aircraft from Australia, three Type-209 class submarines from South Korea, one Dutch Sigma class missile frigate and 10 Russian Su-27 fighters and Su-30 fighters. Malaysia added two Scorpene class submarines and 18 Russian Su-30 fighters to its inventory. US-Philippines maintain cooperative relationship under the mutual defence treaty and military assistance agreement. Philippines has added two Hamilton-class US frigates. Singapore supports the US presence in the Asia-Pacific and permits use of its military facilities. Singapore has deployed US littoral combat ships and added six French Formidable class frigates, two Swedish Archer class submarines, 24 US made F-15 fighters to its military might and participates in the F-35 Joint Strike Fighter Program. [17]

Vietnam and China have been asserting their territorial rights. China has expressed its objections to the other activities in South China Sea. Vietnam is strengthening its relationship with the US and India. India-Vietnam strategic partnership and expanded defence cooperation does not augur well with China. Vietnam has added six Russian Kilo class Submarines, two Gepard class frigates to its Naval fleet and has concluded a contract to purchase a total of 20 Su-30 fighters from Russia.[18]

Myanmar

China is an important partner for Myanmar. China has provided military equipment in addition to economic and infrastructural support to Myanmar. However, of late Myanmar is strengthening its cooperative relationship with India both in economic and military areas and has improved its relationship with the US. China's engagement with Myanmar continues hither-to-fore.

Indian Sub-Continent and IOR

Another contender, competitor and threat to China in South Asia is India. India is considered a threat by China for its continued support to the Tibetan cause and Dalai Lama and its potential in fostering instability in Tibet. India threatens China's core interest of territorial integrity and sovereignty. India's democracy challenges the CCP's format of governance. China is concerned that India's dominance over the SLOCs in the IOR can hurt China's trade and energy flow. In addition, as an emerging Nation, India could challenge China in the region and affect Chinese economic development.

India is viewed as a challenger to China's influence in Asia, a troublesome intruder in South China Sea, an impediment to Chinese interests in the IOR and is also amongst the group of Nations who are colluding with the US to encircle China. Not resolving the border issue, a 'creeping assertiveness' on the line of actual control (LAC) and rhetoric of historical claims are leverages to coerce India to give up on the Tibetan issue and to re-evaluate India's growing strategic proximity to the US. China has been enhancing relationships with India's neighbours - Pakistan, Bangladesh, Myanmar and Sri Lanka.

Ingress and egress routes to the Indian Ocean are within 1000 nm from the Indian Coast. India can influence the sea lanes, from Africa, the Gulf region, all the way to South Asia. This is a matter of concern to China whose Energy supply transits through the IOR. China had been making preparations to enter into the IOR; she has setup bases in the region and has increased involvement in the counter-piracy operations off Somalia. With the development of assets at Hambantota, Gwadar, Sittwe, Chittagong etc China could have formidable presence in the region.

Pakistan continues to remain a not-so-friendly neighbour of India since 1947. However, its economic and military dependency on China has been high and the relationship strong. Over time China has invested in her relationship with Pakistan. Pakistan plans to lease out the strategically important Gilgit-Baltistan region to China for 50 years. This would enable China to extend to the oil and mineral rich land of Afghanistan and Iran, as also to extend her reach to the Arabian coast across Pakistan to its port at Gwadar. The Chinese occupation of Tibet and Aksai Chin have given her control over Tibet and southern Xinjiang, and have provided options to develop land corridors on either flanks of India through Pakistan and Myanmar.

Central Asian Republics

The five landlocked Central Asian Republics (CAR) countries are endowed with natural resources including energy resources. Quest for energy as well as desire to jointly handle extremist elements have got China and CAR countries closer. China has been able to transform the regional dynamics by engaging with the region in geo-energy politics and enhancing geo-economic integration.

US in Asia Pacific

US has been viewing Chinese military transformation with concern. China's Anti Access / Area Denial (A2/AD) preparations, which China refers to as 'Counter Intervention Operations' pose a strategic challenge to the US forces in the region.[19] Hillary Clinton articulated the importance of Asia-Pacific stating that the investments by American companies, freedom of navigation in the South China Sea, countering the proliferation effort of North Korea and ensuring the transparency in the military activities of the region's key players as main strategic objectives of the US. Her strategy for Asia-Pacific has six guidelines; strengthen bilateral security alliances, deepen relationship with emerging powers, including with China and Vietnam; engage with multilateral institutions, expand trade and investment, forge broad-based military presence, and advance democracy and human rights. Treaty alliances with Japan, South Korea, Australia, the Philippines and Thailand are noted as the fulcrum of strategic turn to the Asia–Pacific.[20]

Boost to the US thrust in Asia-Pacific was with the relocation of US Marines in Darwin, Australia and the military engagements with South Korea and Japan, much to the discomfiture of the Chinese. India and US moving closer in defence cooperation, added to China's worries. US has plans to deploy 60 percent of her naval assets in the Western Pacific and in the Indian Ocean, and she may secure/further build upon military bases in the Subic Bay, Clark Air Base (Philippines), Okinawa (Japan), and Darwin (Australia), besides deployments in Indonesia, Singapore and Thailand. US has even evinced interest in the Cam Ranh Bay Port (Vietnam). China fears that this would not only strengthen the combat potential of US bases but will also create an imbalance in the force structure, with tilt in favour of US. The US-Australia joint defence arrangement for intelligence collection, ballistic missiles, early warning, submarine and satellite based communication as well as US-New Zealand defence cooperation seem to justify Chinese apprehensions .

The US follows a 'Hub and Spoke' strategy which envisages using Guam in the Pacific Ocean and Diego Garcia in the Indian Ocean as the two hubs, and these operating bases are expected to act as the rim in the two oceans from where the US can spoke out forces.[21] The Carrier Battle Groups (CBG) and attack submarines can be deployed to choke the strategic straits in the Indian Ocean, Strait of Malacca, Strait of Makassar etc and threaten China's freedom of navigation and use of SLOCs. Therefore, China finds this Asia Pivot Strategy highly provocative and a threat to its core interests in the Asia-Pacific. The Japanese White Paper on Defence, 'Defence of Japan –2013',[22] has diagrammatically depicted the recent trends of US in the region (refer Figure 1).

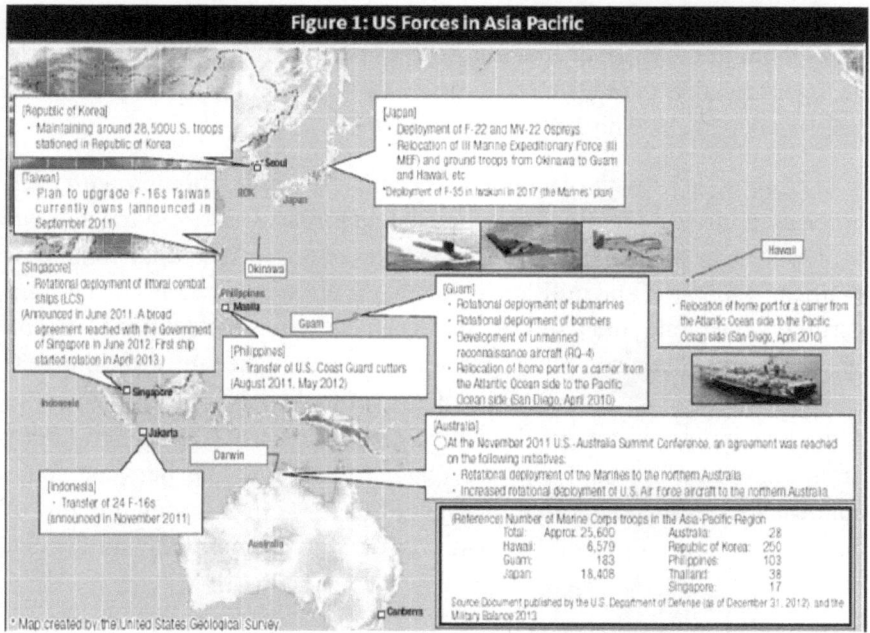

China's Concerns

Chinese threat perceptions have so far indicated that the US continues to be the primary threat for China. From being a supporter of China's integration into the global order in the 90s, the US has come to be viewed as the fundamental obstacle to China's continued ascent in global politics.[23] This is not merely because of the threat the US poses to the core interest of maintaining territorial integrity due to its opposition to the reintegration of Taiwan by force, but also increasingly due to the perception that the US actively seeks to curtail China's strategic manoeuvrability. US is seen as the facilitator and motivator for the China containment move in Asia. US relations with Japan and South Korea, its military engagement with South East Asia and its growing relationship with India are all seen as part of a larger strategy to reduce China's strategic space.[25] The motivation for these American designs is the belief that China's rapid development has unsettled the US. The US forces in the Asia Pacific are as given in Tables 1, 2 and 3.

Analysis of the US Forces deployed in Asia-Pacific indicates that US has key elements for its forces deployed in the area for strategic lift and quick deployment. The forces can position to contain Chinese forces and 'box' them in the rings of first and second island chains. The forces could be operationally deployed for support of Korean, Japanese or Taiwan contingency at short notice.

Chinese look with dismay at the current security situation with each of the core interest identified by China being threatened to varying degrees by US and its allies. The core interests are being affected by alliances-political, economic and military, being put in place by the US and coalition partners. The deployment of US Marines in Darwin is considered by China as a military buildup and force positioning to contain her and is detrimental to her interests. The arc of democracies formed by US, Japan, Australia and India is interpreted by the Chinese as a construct of an anti-China grouping. Thus, China views the quadrilateral dialogue between these countries with disdain. Apart from its military implications this arc of democratic countries has the potential to activate a democratic movement in China or Tibet independence movement.

Chinese leadership has been realistic in its assessment of the situation and her ability to catch up with the US. Deng Xiaoping correctly estimated PLA's inability to catch up with the US even in the next 20 years and beyond as US military would not lie idle but would progress from where it is and hence maintain its technological and operational lead over China. Thus, to take on its potential adversary, the US, China has to fall back on asymmetric warfare capabilities as counter measure and deterrence initiative. The Chinese, experts on stratagem, focused on development of Shashoujian weapons by which 'inferior' China could defeat 'superior' US in case of conflict.

Endnotes

1. China's National Defence, White Paper, Beijing PRC; Information Office of the State Council of the People's Republic of China, 27 July 1998, pp11.

2. Bates Gill, Michael Green, Kiyoto Tsuji, William Watts, "Strategic Views on Asian Regionalism- Survey Results and Analyses" Centre for Strategic and International Studies, Washington DC, 2009 accessed at <http://csis.org/files/media/csis/pubs/090217_gill_stratviews_web.pdf>

3. China's National Defence, White Paper ,Beijing PRC; Information Office of the State Council of the People's Republic of China, 2002. "The capabilities of the US to influence global affairs and the regional environment being of concern to China, compel her to follow a policy to counter US hegemony in the region and place measures that would prevent her 'containment' by US and its allies. Chinese consider that "the old international political and economic order, which is unfair and irrational, has yet to be changed fundamentally. Economic development of the world is materially unbalanced….the developing countries have gained less from the economic globalization process….Democracy in international relations remains elusive, and there are new manifestations of hegemonism and power politics … Rapid and drastic changes are taking place in the military field around the world, and a new serious disequilibrium has occurred in the balance of military power… Traditional security problems left over from history are yet to be resolved, and new ones have appeared."

4. Rukmani Gupta, National Interests and Threat Perceptions: Exploring the Chinese Discourse, IDSA publications.

5. Ka Po Ng, Interpreting China's Military Power: Doctrine makes readiness, Rutledge

6. Rukmani Gupta, National Interests and Threat Perceptions: Exploring the Chinese Discourse, IDSA publications.

7. "Senior Chinese Official calls on U.S. to respect China's core national interests", Xinhua, July 29, 2009 at news.xinhuanet.com/English/2009-07/29content_1179 1654.htm (Accessed on 15 July2010)

8. The Chinese consider themselves as victims of '100 years of shame and humiliation' at the hands of Western powers and the Japanese. They believe that China was invaded, divided, humiliated and weakened by these external powers, until Mao Zedong re-unified China, and founded PRC. This historical period has left a deep impression on the perceptions and national identity of the Chinese. There is hatred for the Japanese in the Chinese hearts as the stories of Japanese cruelties still sustain. The Chinese government, with the making of Nanjing War museum, has instutionalised hatred against the Japanese. The Author noticed a large number of tear filled eyes and 'I hate Japanese' utterances by local Chinese, including the tour guide, during his visit to the Nanjing War Museum. Author considers the spirit of 'Nationalism' is kept burning in the hearts of its citizen by repeated utterance of "period of humiliation" by the Communist Party, and by creation of such memorials. The Party indirectly conveys to the citizens that the Communist Party was the saviour, and continues to be the saviour of China.

9 BBC News Business, China's Economic Growth Rate Stabilizes at 7.7%, www.bbc.co.uk

10 China's National Defence, White Paper, Beijing PRC; Information Office of the State Council of the People's Republic of China,2013

11 Ministry of Foreign Affairs, PRC on its website has posted the issue of divergence with Japan stating Guanghualiao, Kyoto, Japan used to be the students' dormitory, its 5 floors and 1 basement covering an area of 2,130 square meters was taken on rent by Chinese students in the World War II." In May 1950, the Taiwan 'mission' in Japan purchased the estate by the public funds from selling off the properties that Japanese army plundered in the War of Aggression against China. In December 1952, Taiwan 'Embassy to Japan' signed the purchasing contract with the former owner of the estate and registered it under the name of 'the Republic of China' on June 1961. ... After the normalization of the bilateral relations, it should be returned to the PRC and Taiwan should assist in changing its registered name accordingly. It should be noted that Guanghualiao is not just a civil lawsuit but a political case and concerns the legal rights of Chinese government, as well as the basic principles of bilateral relations".

12 Defence Of Japan – 2013, 'Security Environment Surrounding Japan' p1

13 A Taiwanese Official told Author that enhanced tourism and trade provide opportunity for 'Mainland Chinese' to see a 'better system of living'. He stated that a large number of Mainland tourist have 'sleepy dark eyes next morning' after staying awake the entire night watching local TV channels 'criticism of the leadership and government', which is unbelievable and astonishing to them.

14 On the security dilemmas of several Southeast Asian countries vis-à-vis China see Richard A. Bitzinger, "The China Syndrome: Chinese Military Modernization and the Rearming of Southeast Asia" RSIS Papers No. 126 May 2007 Singapore

15 Lu Fanghua, "An Analysis of US involvement in the South China Sea Dispute", Contemporary International Relations, 2010.

16 Rukmani Gupta, National Interests and Threat Perceptions: Exploring the Chinese Discourse, IDSA publications.

17 Adapted from data given in the Japanese White Paper on Defence, Defence Of Japan – 2013

18 Ibid

19 U.S. Office of Secretary of Defence, Quadrennial Defence Review Report, February 2010

20 Hillary Clinton, Remarks at FP's Transformational Trends Forum, 30 Nov 2012.

21 Donald E. Weatherbee, Political Change in Southeast Asia: Challenges for U.S. Strategy,2007

22 Defence Of Japan – 2013, 'Security Environment Surrounding Japan'

23 Wang Jisi, "zhongmeiguanxi de fazhanq U Shiyuzhengceyuanyin (Development trends and causes of China-US relations)", Dangdaiyatai, 3, 2009, pp. 6-22 as mentioned by Rukmani Gupta, National Interests and Threat Perceptions :Exploring the Chinese Discourse, IDSA publications

24 NiuXin Chun, "zhongmeizhanluehuxi: gainian, wentijitiaozhan (China-US strategic mutual trust: concepts, issues and challenges)", Xiandaiguojiguanxi, 3, 2010, pp. 1-3 as mentioned by Rukmani Gupta, National Interests and Threat Perceptions :Exploring the Chinese Discourse, IDSA publications

25 Feng Zhao Kui, "Jianlunzhongmeiboyi dui zhongriguanxi de yingxiang (On implications of Sino-US game on Sino-Japan relations)", Riben Xueli, 6, 2010, pp. 3-16 as mentioned by Rukmani Gupta, National Interests and Threat Perceptions :Exploring the Chinese Discourse, IDSA publications

Evolution of the Assassin's Mace

Specialised warfare leads to Victory, and may not be transmitted beforehand.
—**Sun Tzu**[1]

Historically . . . absolute superiority is present at the end, but is rare at the beginning of a war or campaign.
—**Mao Zedong**[2]

…… although the other side may be strong, they are not strong in all things; they have some weaknesses, and our side may be weak, but we are not weak in all things; we have some strength.

—**Colonel Yu Guohua**[3]

Chinese planners had predicted that China's military strength was in the numbers of uniformed soldiers held and their main task was to fight an enemy face-to-face or occupy territory. The sudden collapse of the Soviet Union, the Gulf Wars, exposure to revolution in military affairs (RMA) and US engagements across the Globe had a major impact on Chinese defence planners. There was a realisation that PLA's approach to warfare and concept of operations needed to undergo a change, a major transformation. PLA had not fought since 1979 and had no military experience in the transforming war fighting techniques that were being witnessed across the globe, metamorphosing the Chinese military was thus a herculean task. Mao Zedong had advocated "learn by doing', which was neither possible nor do-able due to China's efforts for economic growth and the global environment.[4]

Chinese planners chose next closest possible option to learn by doing, they analysed other people's war, the wars that had been fought between different Nations and did not involve China, to examine the strategies employed, technologies developed and focused on the strengths and weaknesses of the contestants. These wars helped the Chinese to not only analyse the future in war fighting trends but also enabled them to assess their toughest potential adversary US' weaknesses and evolve strategies to defeat the US in case of conflict.

For a Nation on path to be a Great Power tomorrow and choosing development and economic growth over military might, enhancement of asymmetric warfare, which has been part of its strategic culture, seemed the most effective choice. Accordingly, China chose to integrate asymmetric warfare capabilities as its deterrence and contingency strategy. Chinese military strategists made systematic time lines to develop China's military might and evolved a time phased approach to develop asymmetries in warfare. The asymmetrical development was given priority over the military modernisation program. Asymmetry in war fighting could be dissimilarities in either organisation or structure or in equipment and its usage, or in war-fighting doctrines and strategies of the armed forces. PLA incorporated these asymmetries in plans and focussed on application of force against relative weaknesses of the adversary.

China's war-fighting history has recorded evidences of use of asymmetry in warfare, prominent being the construction of the Great Wall by the Ming Dynasty, Human Wave attacks during the Korean War, integration of Special Operation Forces, Rapid Reaction Forces in the concepts of military operations etc. 'The Three Warfares concept' which seeks to gain advantage by use of psychological, media and legal warfare is yet another asymmetry China seeks in the current century.The Three Warfares concept uses its three components as given below [5]:-

(a) Psychological Warfare seeks to undermine an enemy's ability to conduct combat operations through operations aimed at deterring, shocking, and demoralizing enemy military personnel and supporting civilian populations.

(b) Media Warfare is aimed at influencing domestic and international public opinion to build support for China's Military actions and dissuade an adversary from pursuing actions contrary to China's interest.

(c) Legal Warfare uses international and domestic law to claim the legal high ground or assert Chinese interests. Legal warfare is also intended to build international support and manage possible political repercussions of China's Military actions.

Shashoujian- the Assassin's Mace

To offset the primacy of regional and extra regional powers in Asia Pacific, the Chinese strategists worked to incorporate asymmetrical operational facets into the principles of war-fighting. Chinese chose to evolve a combat disruptive strategy that seeks to build its strengths to exploit military weaknesses of the enemy - a strategy by which an inferior, could strike at the weaknesses of superior adversary,and negate the superior's strength and capacity. General Fu Quanyou, Vice Chairman, People's Republic of China (PRC), gave clear directions for development of Shashoujian.[6]

'We must lose no time in developing and building "Shashoujian", strengthening military theoretical research, plans and preparation for military struggles, increase effort to acquire scientific and technical knowledge, increasing the scientific and technological drilling of troops, improve construction for war preparedness and study and practice task specific methods of operation in order to comprehensively improve our army's ability to fight combined operations under high-technology conditions.'

To correct the perceived gap in combat primacy Chinese revisited "Shashoujian", an ancient Chinese strategy, which promotes employment of weapons that can overcome a far more powerful adversary as discussed above. Shashoujian (Assassin's Mace) origin lies in the ancient Chinese folklore, which recounts how a hero wielding a 'surprise weapon' managed to overcome a far more powerful adversary. As per the folklore, "Shashoujian" was a club with which the "assassin" was incapacitated, suddenly and totally. Since then, it has come to mean in Chinese military strategy the capacity to rapidly and decisively seize the initiative and turn the tide to one's advantage when confronting a conventionally superior foe.[7] Three Chinese characters form the term Shashoujian. These three characters are sha, meaning kill, shou meaning hand, jian meaning sword or mace, and when together considered they form the term, 'The Assassin's Mace'.

A Shashoujian or the Assassin's Mace, is expected to induce a shock and awe effect when used against an adversary, would have a massive destructive potential and would shatter the enemy, or his will to fight. Thus, the focus of the attacks would be on the adversary's weaknesses with the aim to affect his mind, paralyze him, make his capacity less effective and render his advance capabilities useless.

Combat disruptive technologies being evolved by China are powerful enough to deter a superior adversary. In line with the stratagem "inferior can defeat the superior", China apparently seeks to combine both the Chinese tradition of strategic thought and Shashoujian with the technologies of the modern world. Jiang Zemin is said to have directed that China should first concentrate on Shashoujian weapons to safeguard China's national security, territorial integrity and to oppose hegemony in today and tomorrow's world. Shashoujian weapons can thus be considered as China's trump card or a magic wand that would further China's National Interest.

Assassin's Mace concept impacts not only the evolution of military strategy, weapons development program but also aids in formulation of concepts for war-fighting, plans for conduct of offensive and defensive operations and evolution of deterrence strategies. Shashoujian thus influences grand strategy, national security policy and military affairs. Shashoujian through a war fighting strategy is being effectively used by China as a deterrence tool.

Assassin's Mace or the Shashoujian weapons are usually developed in secret, from unknown technologies, and their concept of operations if undisclosed, has a greater shock and awe effect. In Shashoujian weapons employment, the element of surprise is essential and in their execution, the vital weakness of the enemy has to be addressed to precipitate defeat.[8] Chinese believe that for successful employment of the Assassin's Mace weapons or Shashoujian against a superior adversary requires good intelligence and correct assessment of the adversary's strategy, tactics, weapons, platforms, and systems. Identification of the Centers of Gravity (COG) within the enemy's military structure is of paramount importance. Once strengths and weaknesses have been identified and assessed, the strengths can be avoided, and the weaknesses can be targeted for attack using Shashoujian.[9]

The Assassin's Mace weapon program comprises a new PLA weapons development and acquisition program using both low and high end technologies. Chinese strategists consider that Shashoujian could be a relatively simple weapon, such as a novel type of naval mine, or very complex high tech equipment such as a new supersonic missile that cannot be intercepted.[10] Senior Colonel Yang Zhibo of PLAAF Command College, considers that Shashoujian can be "weapon systems or an equipment" and/or a certain type of "combat method." In fact, it can be whatever PLA needs to win future local wars under modern high-tech conditions. He has opined that "weapons systems or equipment" are the systems needed to deal with the enemy's electronic warfare and information warfare, and to counter every type of weapon and equipment the enemy can use for firepower attack. Shashoujian "combat methods" include attacking using different types of weapons, such as early warning aircraft, stealth aircraft, and cruise missiles, as well as the combat principles to deal with different situations.[11] An analysis of Chinese strategies to counter US brings out another facet in use of Assassin's Mace. Shashoujian are likely to be integrated with timelines and phases of battle commencing from 'Prior to War stage', 'Pre-emptive Strike' and there-after in actual conduct of operations.

In line with the stratagem "inferior can defeat the superior", Chinese apparently seek to combine both the Chinese tradition of strategic thought and Shashoujian with the technologies of the modern world. PLA strategists stress on the need of conducting Shashoujian strikes on critical infrastructure that supports military operations. Cyber-attacks could commence even before hostilities commence, while physical destruction could be a part of pre-emptive strike. As a rule, Shashoujian weapons are high technology weapons developed in secrecy. However, China regularly, prior to visits of high level dignitaries, show-cases one or more of its innovation on technological achievement like firing of Anti Satellite Missile, disclosures of its stealth fighter etc. An unstated signal is given, "We have weapons that would offset your military force advantages, don't mess with us". Thus, the strategy focuses on use of Shashoujian as a deterrence tool. Some of the targets identified by Chinese military scholars for Shashoujian strikes include Command and Control Centers, systems and networks, early warning and intelligence systems, remote sensing platforms (specifically unmanned aerial vehicles and reconnaissance satellites), and military logistics systems,[12] support infrastructure as also civil structures.

Chinese military experts consider that for building a Shashoujian, China must first evolve a plan of complete weapon development and not just one or two advance weapons. The process of evolving Assassin's Mace weapons will be long and difficult but needs to evolve systematically by all the Services. Shashoujian would be an all-army, all-location, composite land, sea, and air system and would need to be a Chinese program since it cannot be purchased from abroad.[13] Hence, Shashoujian Weapons could be Land Based Shashoujian (LBS), Air Based Shashoujian (ABS), Oceanic Strike Shashoujian (OSS) and Space Based Shashoujian (SBS).

Shashoujian forces must serve as a credible deterrent and an effective tool in pre-emption and must also be able to survive initial attacks by a superior adversary to ensure the PLA's ability to achieve victory through devastating counterstrikes. Choice of weapon, tactics of employment, timings of a strike and stratagem are essential in elements of the Assassin's Mace. A number of targets have been identified by China which they plan to engage by Assassin's Mace weapons with the hope of crippling the adversary. These Shashoujian weapons have been incorporated in PLA war-fighting strategies. The weapons and the stages at which they may aid PLA in war are deliberated in the next Chapter.

China's understanding of way ahead is that conventional weapons of today are no longer capable of dealing with complex electronic equipment and advanced technologies of the future battlefield. Therefore, China considers it imperative to build up a new generation of weapons using current and futuristic technologies. China launched its "863 Program" in response to the US Strategic Defence Initiative in 1986. Products of the 863 Program include space and airborne synthetic aperture radars, unmanned deep-diving submarines, unmanned micro-aircraft, gas-cooled nuclear reactors, space launch vehicles, satellites and the Assassin's Mace weapons. Accordingly, a number of high technology military programs, at research facilities and universities, were started by China and these are involved in developing high technology military-ware.

Endnotes

1. Thomas Huynh, The Art of War, Jaico Publishing House

2. Collected Works of Mao Zedong, Beijing, Renmin Chubanbshe, 1964.

3. Jason E. Bruzdzinski, quoting Yu Guohua from "On Turning a Strong Force Into Weak and Vice Versa in a Local High-Tech War," Zhongguo Junshi Kexue, May 20, 1996, in FBIS, In Demystifying Shashoujian: China's "Assassin's Mace" Concept

4. Andrew Scobell, David Lai, Roy Kamphausen, Chinese Lessons From Other Peoples' Wars, Strategic Studies Institute Book, November 2011

5. Timothy A Walton, China's Three Warfare, Delex consulting Studies and Analysis, January 2012

6. Jason E. Bruzdzinski, in his article Demystifying Shashoujian: China's "Assassin's Mace" Concept, has quoted General Fu Quanyou as given in FBIS document, "Deepen the Study of Characteristics and Laws of High-Technology Local War and Raise the Standard of Guidance for Winning High-Technology Local Wars of the Future, Zhongguo Junshi Kexue, February 20, 1999, pp 6-1.

7. http://en.wikipedia.org/wiki/Assassin's_Mace

8. Richard D Fisher, China's Military Modernisation, Building for Regional and Global Reach, Greenwood Publishing, 2008

9. Jason E. Bruzdzinski ,Demystifying Shashoujian: China's "Assassin's Mace" Concept, at www.books.google.co.uk

10. Richard D Fisher, China's Military Modernisation, Building for Regional and Global Reach, Greenwood Publishing, 2008

11. Report, China Developing Super Electromagnet Pulse Bomb To Use In War Against US, http://www.examiner.com/article/china-developing-super-electromagnet-pulse-bomb-to-use-war-against-u-s

12. Jason E. Bruzdzinski ,Demystifying Shashoujian: China's "Assassin's Mace" Concept

13. Report, China Developing Super Electromagnet Pulse Bomb To Use In War Against US, http://www.examiner.com/article/china-developing-super-electromagnet-pulse-bomb-to-use-war-against-u-s

Shashoujian in War Fighting Strategies

Even if we could modernize our military equipment in the next 10 or 20 years, compared to our enemies, our weapons would still be inferior. We are moving forward, but our enemies are not asleep either. Therefore, by that time, if we have to fight, we will still be the weak trying to defeat the strong.

—**Deng Xiaoping**

Chinese are aware that despite the considerable progress PLA has made in recent years it still lags behind the US military in terms of technology, doctrine, training, and experience and that any conflict against the US military will pose extreme challenges. Deng Xiaoping opined that if China continues normal process of modernisation, China will continue to be a step or two behind its potential adversary. To defeat a technologically superior adversary the PLA would need to focus on devising strategies that maximize China's relative strengths and with the use of 'stratagems' and Shashoujian, create opportunities to exploit US weaknesses. Thus for its war fighting strategies, PLA would not seek to confront the US military in a force-on-force battle but would seek to strike decisively at US vulnerabilities using Assassin's Mace. The strikes, aimed at the COG of the adversary, would aim to render ineffective the enemy's war fighting capability. Thus, PLA chose to integrate Shashoujian in its 'War Fighting Strategies', employing the Assassin's Mace in a time phased manner. This strategy would also aid PLA in its contest with India and is discussed in the last chapter.

Prior to evolving a strategy for its forces, it is imperative to holistically examine the adversary's capability - the strengths and the weaknesses. Accordingly, Chinese analysed recent wars that the US has been engaged in to arrive at lessons for itself and the way ahead for its military forces. Amongst the various lessons learnt was one important understanding that American influence and presence in the region is not always stabilizing[1]. Chinese planners stated that US military operations in Middle East solidify these views. Hence, for Chinese strategists, the US enhanced presence in China's periphery would increase instability in the region and PLA should be prepared for a conflict. In case of a conflict with the US, China's strategy would be to frustrate the adversary's strategic intentions, undermine its resolve and determination to get in a conflict thereby prevent US from engaging in the type of war it wants to fight. To be able to do so, it would be necessary for China to inflict unacceptable casualties and costs to the US.

Chinese strategy towards a potential conflict with the US arises from a belief that even an adversary with superior weapons, technology, and equipment will not be able to maintain absolute superiority in all respects. It would provide China an opportunity to strike, using stratagem and Shashoujian. Chinese expect that the conflict would take place within a specific geographic limit at its periphery and would provide the PLA ample opportunities to offset the US' technological advantages in land, air, sea and space warfare.[2] The Assassin's Mace weaponry would have a far reaching effect in China's future wars.

China's Likely Strategy for Operations

Chinese strategy for operations using Shashoujian can be divided into three distinct time phased stages — Strategies prior to declaration of hostilities, Pre-emptive strikes and the actual conduct of war. Broadly, the operations could be conducted as given below:-

(a) China's likely strategy against the US would be that of time phased stages where the PLA would disrupt US battle networks by degrading or destroying the US satellite constellation in concert with coordinated cyber and electronic warfare attacks.

(b) The cyber war would commence prior to hostilities, while physical attacks using Shashoujian weapons could commence as pre-emptive strikes. Directed energy weapons, missiles of various types and even space based assets could be employed for these strikes.

(c) PLA would use salvoes of missiles and precision guided munitions (PGMs), Unmanned Combat Platform (UCP) like UCAVs and underwater weapons to strike at US and allied targets, such as forward air bases, CBG and key logistics capabilities with the aim to deny strategic spaces and compel US to operate from longer ranges.

(d) China has evolved a strategy of key point strikes where the objective of a strike is to neutralize and degrade systems and vital linkages, and to defeat a technologically superior adversary's Command, Control and early warning systems. This could cripple and blind US forces and cloud the mind and confuse military commanders at all levels.

(e) China would aim to render non-operational the US CBGs and the US aircraft at forward bases by use of Shashoujian. Once the US aircraft are unable to sortie or are destroyed, PLA would gain freedom of maneuver for its air force and naval forces, and focus on achieving its military and political goals.

Strategies Prior To Declaration of Hostilities

Chinese strategists understand that success against the US military depends on China's ability to avoid a direct confrontation with US forces in a traditional, force-on-force battle. In an interview with the newspaper China Youth Daily, a PLA Senior Colonel compared an attempt by China to directly take on the US in a high technology conflict as being akin to "throwing an egg against a rock".[3] Chinese consider that Shashoujian weapons would be critical for deterrence. Thus, for China it is important that the US is aware that China has and is further evolving its Shashoujian. The showcasing and testing of high tech weapons just ahead of foreign dignitaries visit[4] to China or arising from irks felt by China[5] are but strategies to enhance deterrence by impregnating potential adversary leaderships mind with a sense of fear of Shashoujian and the adverse impact it would have. Show-casing of anti-satellite capabilities, flight of a stealth bomber, lasing of US satellites from ground based laser etc, at carefully chosen time, are but extensions of this strategy. The Assassin's Mace shock and awe strikes can restrict the war at the initial stages. Shashoujian would enable graduated escalation and provide opportunity for favourable political settlement preventing an all-out war.

Many Chinese strategists argue that the US would not have been able to win the Kosovo and the Gulf Wars without the assistance and support of its coalition partners.[6] For the US, the most critical aspect of dependence on allied support was the requirement of access to forward bases. US forces would have difficulty launching multiple waves of quick and sudden air strikes if they are forced to rely on second- and third-line airfields and aircraft carriers to launch air strikes and their overall operational capabilities would get greatly reduced.[7] Chinese draw from these the importance of minimizing possibilities of US alliances with the Nations located in China's periphery, and use the strategies that create the perception that joining hands with US may not be a good strategy in the long term. Militarily, the Shashoujian weaponry re-enforces this idea as it goes to suggest that US would be kept at bay at the time of need by the medium and long range ballistic missiles with terminally guided maneuverable warheads, supersonic and accurate cruise missiles, armed with electromagnetic pulse or nuclear warheads. The loss of face by the US in the Spratly Island dispute and issues relating to ADIZ over Senkaku Island sows in the minds of US allies[8] the seeds of doubt that US may not be such a reliable partner when things go astray.[9]

Chinese have assessed that there is intolerance to body bags in domestic US population opinion. Thus the US leadership confronts several domestic factors that restrict their military and diplomatic options, like partisan politics, potential public opposition, a highly critical media, and an assertive Congress. Chinese writers frequently argue that these domestic pressures are functions of an almost total unwillingness on the part of US leadership and public to accept casualties in military conflicts. A 'Liberation Army Daily' article asserts that the US public is 'abnormally sensitive' about military casualties and that its tolerance for casualties is continuing to decline. Once casualties occur in a war, there are domestic antiwar outcries and the US citizens call to end hostilities.[10] Chinese strategists consider that the US aversion to casualties could be exploited by delivering a sudden pre-emptive strike aimed at causing a large number of US military casualties, sowing doubt and discontent among the US population and potentially forcing the withdrawal of US forces. The Chinese strategists consider that this can be achieved by pre-emptive strikes on large military targets using Assassin's Mace weapons. Destruction of the Aircraft Carrier on its way to deployment by strike by missiles like DF21[11], cruise missiles and UCPs like old fighter aircraft (converted into explosive laden UAV for kamikaze attack on Carrier), would cause large human casualties and hence is amongst one of the choice targets for Shashoujian strikes.

Conduct Of Operations

Chinese strategists emphasize achieving victory through surprise by striking at an unexpected time and an unanticipated place, disguising one's own intent well.[12] The objective of disguising one's intent can be achieved through camouflage, deception, feint, gainful use of weather and by carefully timing the strikes. Though it is more difficult to disguise one's intent under modern conditions, Chinese experts have stated that modern campaign practice have proved that it is still possible to take the enemy by surprise through excellent stratagem and use of modern concealment technologies and smart camouflage of physical and electronic signatures of equipment. Chinese doctrinal material defines strategic deception as luring the other side into developing misperceptions and establishing for oneself a strategically advantageous position by producing various kinds of false phenomena in an organised and planned manner with the smallest cost in manpower and material. The main driver of China's strategic deception is enhanced information warfare that revolves around Psychological Warfare, Electronic Warfare, Deception, Computer Network Attacks and Precision Strike Warfare - all are the components of China's Shashoujian philosophy.

Chinese analysts consider that the US has difficulty in establishing clear military superiority at the outset of a conflict despite the number of bases and alliances it has across the globe. Closely related to the challenges of rapid deployment are issues of logistics and supply. During the Gulf War it took only about 14 hours for US aircraft to travel from the continental US to the region, but it took 14 days for many ships to reach the Persian Gulf.[13] The total time required for preparation was five months, long enough for Iraq to have taken some sort of action to disrupt the US deployment to the theater, had Baghdad decided to launch a preemptive strike.[14] According to Chinese analysts when US forces operate at great distances, supply lines are long and ensuring effective logistics support is extremely challenging. A Liberation Army Daily article argues, that "in a high tech local war, a belligerent (army) which adopts a passive defensive strategy and launches no offensive against the enemy is bound to fold its hands and await destruction". Thus, pre-emptive strikes would be favourable to China.[15] Firepower assaults, electronic warfare, and psychological warfare, Special Forces and Shashoujian strikes would play a key role in any preemptive strike. Special Forces units would "infiltrate the enemy's rear area to carry out special operations and sabotage, attacking the critical elements and key links of its war making machine everywhere- on land, at sea, and in the air".[16] Thus, it is imperative that China launches a pre-emptive strike before the enemy is able to develop its full combat potential in the war zone. Shashoujian weapons like information warfare tools, ballistic missile, cruise missile assaults, UCP engagements along with simultaneously disruption of communications could result in early closure of war.

China does feel constrained by the island chains that ring her, however, geography favours her as any major conventional conflict involving the US will necessitate US bringing its forces across the Pacific, Indian, and/or Atlantic Oceans, and thereafter logistically sustain them. In so doing, the US will be crossing thousands of kilometers of SLOC which would easily be engaged by Chinese submarines lying in ambush, and Chinese Shashoujian weapons like bottom-rising sea mines, super-cavitating under water weapons, and supersonic cruise missiles etc. The air corridors above these sea lanes would be threatened by advanced air defence systems aboard Stealth destroyers. CBGs, logistic and transport ships and oil tankers would be targeted by such Chinese attacks. The US operational forces and logistics elements in numerous military bases strategically encircling China could be neutralized by Shashoujian weapons and conventional warheads. Thus, the US will be forced by geography to suffer the disadvantages of conducting offensive operations against China.[17] The time phased engagement of US forces with a variety of Shashoujian, at different distances from China's coast line would have catastrophic effects on adversary's operations.

Key points are targets that could have a direct influence on the overall situation of the campaign or produce an overall effect. The PLA's key-point strike concept is based on the premise that all militaries, regardless of how capable or technologically advanced they are possess areas of vulnerability. They include systems, parts, and links vital to the sustaining of the campaign, as well as important force groupings and important battlefield facilities. The objective of key-point strikes is to neutralise the enemy's operational superiority. Command systems are the nerve centers of operations and destruction of the enemy's command system could paralyze the entire campaign system. Hence, crippling the enemy's command system is vital to the destruction of the overall structure. Thus, developing Shashoujian weapons for targeting command and control apparatus is essential. Hence, China has been focusing on the development of various facets of information warfare including Space warfare.

Military information systems comprise complex networks of surveillance and reconnaissance devices, communication facilities, command-and-control facilities and information processing and display equipment. Chinese strategists view information capabilities as an essential component of a military force's strength. Hence, crippling or destroying the enemy's information system can significantly degrade the enemy's combat capabilities by making it "blind," "deaf," and "paralyzed". Hence, Assassin's Mace weapons must cater for neutralizing information systems by use of soft kills attacks like employing Cyber warfare tools to inject malicious worms and viruses, neutralization of adversary satellite constellations or even cause physical destruction of the assets.

Weapons are the teeth of war-fighting. Destroying the enemy's modern weapon systems would degrade its overall combat capabilities and facilitate victory. Hence, China is evolving its Shashoujian weaponry to destroy modern high technology weapons. To increase arsenal in her inventory, China has also focused its efforts towards directed energy weapons which would degrade/destroy adversary's high technology weapons at large distances from China's periphery.

Information Warfare, Space warfare and technologies that aid in conduct of counter-intervention operations are the mainstay of Chinese military modernisation and Assassin's Mace program.

Due to their high operational tempo and consumption of materiel, modern campaigns require extensive logistic support. Damage inflicted on various bases and facilities would put a combatant in a passive position, cause him to undertake a 'logistic pause' or even give up the idea of progressing operations any further. Shashoujian weapons could be used to disrupt adversary's logistic support facilities and replenishment chain.

Chinese strategists recognize that they will not have to achieve a total military victory over the US. Under conditions of local war, political goals will be limited. Thus, China needs to achieve a relative military victory to attain its larger political objectives. Shashoujian would facilitate achievement of these goals.

Counter Intervention Operations

Anti-Access strategy involves any action by an opponent that has the effect of slowing the deployment of friendly forces into a theater, preventing them from operating from certain locations within that theater, or causing them to operate from distances farther from the center of conflict than they would normally prefer.[18] China has prioritized land-based ballistic and cruise missile programs to extend its strike warfare capabilities further from its borders. It is developing and testing several new classes and variants of offensive missiles, forming additional missile units, upgrading older missile systems, and developing methods to counter ballistic missile defences. In addition, silent submarines, UCP, Shashoujian weapons including under water weapons help to achieve anti-access.

China's Anti-Access /Area Denial (A2/AD) strategy or the Counter Intervention Operations aims at preserving and maximizing a country's strategic space through deterrence exercised by strong military capability that is intended to raise the costs of intervention for a potential challenger. Chinese military is expected to take the initiative, achieve surprise and pre-empt the US by its key point integrated strikes which manifest as concentrated, multi-dimensional and multi-spectral attacks on combat, combat support, logistics and Theatre Information Systems.[19] China is pursuing a variety of air, sea, undersea, space and counter-space and Information warfare systems and operational concepts to achieve this capability, moving towards an array of over-lapping multi-layered offensive capabilities extending from China's coast into the Western pacific.[20] China is working on a range of technologies to attempt to counter US and other countries' ballistic missile defence systems, including maneuverable re-entry vehicles (MaRVs), MIRVs, decoys, chaff, jamming, thermal shielding, and anti-satellite (ASAT) weapons. China has strengthened her triad capacity by inducting sea based nuclear missiles. The naval vector consists of SLBM JL-1 (1000+ Km), Jin class (SSBN), SLBM JL 2(7400+ Km) and an anti-ship ballistic missile (ASBM) the DF-21-D which is a variant of DF-21. The DF-21 D has a maneuverable warhead (MaRV)[21] with a range of 2500 km and is capable of targeting a moving aircraft carrier.[22] China's White Paper on Defence 2008 states that one of the priorities for the development of China's Armed Forces is to increase the country's capabilities to maintain maritime, space, and electromagnetic space security.[23]

US concerns of the evolving Chinese A2/AD capabilities find mention in the Annual Report to Congress. It has been brought out that China is improving information and operational security to protect its own information structures and is also developing electronic and information warfare capabilities, including denial and deception, to defeat its adversaries. China's information blockade envisions employment of military and non-military instruments of state power across the battle-space, including in cyberspace and outer space. China is also developing weapons for its entire military to project force further from its coast. Current and projected missile systems allow the PLA to strike regional air bases, logistical facilities and other infrastructure[24].

Counter intervention capabilities are being enhanced by addition of medium and short range ballistic missiles (DF 21s and DF 15s), with terminally guided maneuverable re-entry vehicles with a circular error probability of 10 meters. DF 21s can hit slow moving targets at sea[25] and thus pose a serious threat to deployments of naval platforms. China's adversaries do not have any known viable counter measures in place as of now. Thus, attacks by these missiles can disrupt her adversary's operational plans by its destructive power and have serious implications for India. Advance system of the US Navy like the Aegis missile defence system and the Phalanx Close-in Defence weapons would be susceptible to attack by supersonic cruise missiles launched from PLA submarines,[26] aircraft, surface ships, UCAVs or even common trucks. These missiles, armed with conventional, anti-radiation, thermobaric, or electro-magnetic pulse warheads or even nuclear warheads would be the Shashoujian that will win the war for China in Western Pacific and IOR.

Specially designed to target aircraft carriers, bottom rising, rocket propelled sea mines laid by submarines, can be grouped in clusters to strike the carriers in barrages, to destroy them or/and render them operationally ineffective.[27] These Assassin's Mace weapons can be used at choke points in SLOCs. The IOR provides number of suitable choke points where the

Shashoujian can be used to its full measure. Fleet of old fighter aircraft modified as UCAV fitted with extra fuel tanks and armed with stand-off anti-ship missiles and high explosives can cause the destruction of adversary's naval fleets, logistic bases etc. The UCAV could, after firing off their precision-guided anti-ship missiles on the CBG, finish their mission by dive-bombing onto their targets in "kamikaze" style. India will need to cater for these while planning for operations.

Active Defence

The active defence doctrine is a transformation from Mao's large scale people's land centric war to a high intensity, short duration local war under informationalized conditions. The guiding principle is passivity in external form and appearance but action in internal functioning. The active defence doctrine postulates that one should take defence at the beginning of the enemy's attack and actively take offensive actions to defeat the enemy after he gets exhausted. Therefore, active defence policy necessitates forward positioning, frontier defence, engagement of the enemy at or over the border and potential engagement in conflict beyond China's immediate periphery.[28] The doctrine is essentially pro-active and seeks to take the battle into enemy territory and supports use of Shashoujian and stratagems.

Nuclear Deterrence

China's ancient strategists state that the best military leader wins his objectives without resorting to warfare. This virtue is still respected and practised in the PRC today and directs emphasis on strategy, deterrence, and negotiation over armed conflict. Chinese writing on Shashoujian weapons includes discussion of psychological warfare, requirement for credible deterrence, and negotiation over armed conflict. China's strategic missile forces, PLA's Second Artillery and PLAN strategic submarine fleet are considered as Shashoujian forces. China's military nuclear program has witnessed a steady transition from nuclear defence to minimum credible deterrence. The emphasis currently is on limited nuclear deterrence which entails enhancement in nuclear deterrence to 'assured and survivable' second strike capability.

Conventional Missiles

In the conventional field, the Second Artillery, which had no conventional missiles till 1985, now has the largest conventional missile arsenal in the Asia-Pacific.[29] They also have 200-500 Ground Launched Cruise Missiles. This approach of using concentrated ballistic and cruise missile can be used not only against Taiwan but also against India. The various options of missiles available with PLA are as under:-

(a) Second Artillery has more than a thousand Short-Range Ballistic Missiles (< 1,000 km) and the Second Artillery continues to field advanced variants with improved ranges and more sophisticated payloads.

(b) Medium-Range Ballistic Missiles (MRBM) increase the ranges at which PLA can conduct precision strikes against land targets and naval ships. With a range of 3000 km, MRBM can target ships deployed near the first island chain.

(c) Conventional Intermediate-Range Ballistic Missiles, with ranges upto 5,000 km, increase PLA's capability for near-precision strike out to the second island chain. PLAN, with over-the-horizon (OTH) targeting capability with sky wave and surface wave OTH radars, in conjunction with reconnaissance satellites, can locate targets at great distances from China and thereby support long-range precision strikes.

(d) PLA has air and ground launched Land-Attack Cruise Missiles for stand-off, precision strikes. Air-launched Cruise Missiles include the YJ-63, KD-88 and the CJ-20.

(e) PLAAF has tactical air-to-surface missiles as well as precision-guided munitions including all-weather, satellite-guided bombs, anti-radiation missiles and laser-guided bombs.

(f) PLAN has deployed domestically-produced, ship-launched YJ-62 ASCM; the Russian SS-N-22/Sunburn supersonic ASCM, on China's Sovremenny Class DDGs acquired from Russia; and the Russian SS-N-27B/Sizzler supersonic ASCM[30] on China's Russian-built KILO SS. ASCM variants range from the 1950s-era CSS-N-2 to the modern Russian-made SS-N-22 and SS-N-

27B. China is developing indigenous supersonic cruise missile capability.[31] The pace of ASCM research, development, and production has accelerated over the past decade.

The Missile force serves as a force multiplier and increases the lethality of attacks. The numbers of missile continue to grow indicating the importance China is giving to its missile warfare. Short-Range Ballistic Missiles numbers have increased from being just 30 per cent in 2000 to 50 per cent of Second Artillery's missile systems today. The missiles per launcher have also increased for both the Short-Range Ballistic Missiles and the Ground Launched Cruise Missiles. China has one of the largest arsenals of cruise missiles. The Inter-Continental Ballistic Missiles count has increased from 5 per cent to nearly 14 per cent and may grow further as China develops new variants like the DF 31/31-A and DF-41. New variants have better ranges and maneuverability. The Intermediate-Range Ballistic Missiles have decreased but the 21C and 21D MRBM have increased phenomenally and large numbers of these are being deployed in Tibet.

Logistic System

Launching attacks against the enemy's logistics system is another key element of China's overall strategy for dealing with the US military as discussed earlier in the Chapter. Attacks on the logistics system have anti-access implications and hence, find special consideration by China for engaging with combat disruptive technology weapons. Chinese military writings discuss launching attacks on logistics, transportation, and support facilities to delay the deployment of new US forces to the region and render existing forces in the region less effective or more vulnerable because of a lack of timely supplies of materiel needed for war-fighting.[32] Strategists have stated that US combat forces deploy with very limited supplies, perhaps enough to last for no more than two to five days. The logistics and support requirements of high-technology forces are formidable. Chinese military writers estimate that an aircraft carrier strike group requires replenishment of 60,000 tons of ordinary fuel and 30,000 tons of aviation fuel every four to five days. US has to undertake complex logistics and support operations. Chinese analysts estimate that it can take as much as three to four months for the US to establish a complete logistics and supply network in distant theater of operations.[33] Thus, US' heavy dependence on logistics and support is seen as one of the main vulnerabilities of US forces. Attack by Special Forces, destruction of logistic bases by missiles, prevention of replenishment of logistic dumps, destruction of underway replenishment tankers by super-cavitation underwater weapons and other UCPs are drivers to Shashoujian evolution.

Evolution of Assassin's Mace program is a progressive and continued effort by China. China conceptualized leapfrog development of technologies and its Shashoujian program is evolving from one level to the next. The trends in Assassin's Mace in land, air, sea and space are discussed in the next Chapter.

Endnotes

1. Kurt M. Campbell, Nirav Patel, Richard Weitz, The Ripple Effect: China's Responses to the Iraq War, Center for a New American Security paper, October 2008

2. Roger Cliff, Mark Burles, Michael S. Chase, Derek Eaton, Kevin L. Pollpeter, Entering the Dragon's Lair: Chinese Anti-access Strategies and their Implications for the United States, RAND Corporation 2007

3. Roger Cliff, Mark Burles, Michael S. Chase, Derek Eaton, Kevin L. Pollpeter, Entering the Dragon's Lair: Chinese Anti-access Strategies and their Implications for the United States, RAND Corporation 2007

4. China tested the prototype of its fifth-generation fighter jet Chengdu J-20 during US Defence Secretary Robert Gates visit China. Mr. Gates stated that he definitely did not expect that China would make such a surprise during his visit to the country. (The Japan Times, China tests secret weapon to Robert Gates astonishment http://english.pravda.ru/world/asia/12-01-2011/116493-china_fifth_generation-0/)

5. China's military conducted the first test of a new ground-launched anti-satellite missile that was fired into space and disguised as a space-exploration rocket. The ASAT test comes a week after China protested the release of the Pentagon's annual report on the Chinese military buildup that mentioned Beijing's development of anti-satellite weapons. (Before Its News, China Conducts Test of New Anti-Satellite Missile, http://beforeitsnews.com/war-and-conflict/2013/05/china-conducts-test-of-new-anti-satellite-missile-2446758.html)

6. Andrew Scobell, David Lai, Roy Kamphausen, Chinese Lessons From Other Peoples' Wars, Strategic Studies Institute Book, November 2011

7   Roger Cliff, Mark Burles, Michael S. Chase, Derek Eaton, Kevin L. Pollpeter, Entering the Dragon's Lair: Chinese Anti-access Strategies and their Implications for the United States , 2007

8   Kalha RS, China's ADIZ-A case of Over Reach, www.idsa.in.

9   Brig Vinod Anand, China's new ADIZ over East China Sea, Implications for India, www.vifindia.org

10   Roger Cliff, Mark Burles, Michael S. Chase, Derek Eaton, Kevin L. Pollpeter, Entering the Dragon's Lair: Chinese Anti-access Strategies and their Implications for the United States , 2007

11   Ronald O' Rourke, China Naval Modernization: Implications for US Navy Capabilities – Background and Issues for Congress ,China-United States Economic and Geopolitical Relations, Nova Science Publishers, 2007

12   Roger Cliff, Mark Burles, Michael S. Chase, Derek Eaton, Kevin L. Pollpeter, Entering the Dragon's Lair: Chinese Anti-access Strategies and their Implications for the United States , 2007

13   Andrew Scobell, David Lai, Roy Kamphausen, Chinese Lessons From Other Peoples' Wars, Strategic Studies Institute Book, November 2011

14   Roger Cliff, Mark Burles, Michael S. Chase, Derek Eaton, Kevin L. Pollpeter, Entering the Dragon's Lair: Chinese Anti-access Strategies and their Implications for the United States , 2007

15   Ibid

16   Ibid

17   Victor N Corpus, America's Acupuncture Points, http://www.atimes.com/atimes/China/HJ20Ad01.html

18   Roger Cliff, Mark Burles, Michael S. Chase, Derek Eaton, Kevin L. Pollpeter, Entering the Dragon's Lair: Chinese Anti-access Strategies and their Implications for the United States , 2007

19   Guangqian Peng and Youzhi Yao, Ed, 'Strategic Guidance of High-Tech Local War, The Science of Military Strategy,' Academy of Military Science, Beijing, Jun 2005.

20   Annual report to Congress: Military and Security Developments involving the PRC, 2013.

21   Ibid

22   Victor N Corpus, America's Acupuncture Points, http://www.atimes.com/atimes/China/HJ20Ad01.html

23   China's National Defence, White Paper Beijing PRC; Information Office of the State Council of the People's Republic of China, 2008

24. Annual report to Congress: Military and Security Developments involving the PRC, 2013, as available on the net.

25. Victor N Corpus, America's Acupuncture Points, http://www.atimes.com/atimes/China/HJ20Ad01.html

26. Ibid

27. Ibid

28. David Shambaugh, Modernising China's Military, Progress, Problems and Prospects,University of California Press,2002

29. Annual Report to Congress: Military and Security Developments Involving the People's Republic of China,2013

30. Annual Report To Congress ,Military Power of the People's Republic of China, 2006

31. Ronald O' Rourke, China Naval Modernization: Implications for US Navy Capabilities – Background and Issues for Congress ,China-United States Economic and Geopolitical Relations, Nova Science Publishers, 2007

32. Roger Cliff, MarkBurles, Michael S. Chase, Derek Eaton, Kevin L. Pollpeter, Entering the Dragon's Lair: Chinese Anti-access Strategies and their Implications for the United States , 2007

33. Ibid

Trends in Chinese Assassin's Mace

"Those skilled in warfare make themselves invincible and then wait for the enemy to become vulnerable."
—**Sun Tzu**

"You fight your way and I will fight my way."
— **Mao Zedong**

"After all the humiliations of the past, it is time for China to stand up again in the world."
—**Liang Yan**

The Shashoujian weapons are of major emphasis in the RMA as they are new technological innovations that provide a previously unavailable capability to the PLA. These weapons offer a strategy which is not expected by the adversary and then, suddenly when he encounters the stratagem's execution by his adversary, his thinking and combat abilities freeze with shock, and his vulnerabilities increase. Thus, Assassin's Mace weapons are those weapons which by their first use could cripple or degrade the adversary's ability to react or continue to resist. Tactical nuclear weapons, stealth and counter stealth equipment, hyper velocity vehicles etc could be seen as Assassin's Mace weapons as they would severely limit adversary forces' ability to react and make them vulnerable to attack by PLA forces. Similarly, while in the context of fighting a CBG, the development of an Electro-magnetic Pulse (EMP) weapon and carrier killer missiles are Assassin's Mace of formidable effectiveness and Shashoujian use could significantly degrade the combat potential of the CBG.

The Shashoujian weapons can be used against ground, sea, air and space targets and hence can be classified based on the concept of design and operations. I have classified the Shashoujian weapons in four broad categories in the Book based on operating space in which they are likely to be employed from. Hence, they are classified as Space Based Shashoujian (SBS), Air Based Shashoujian (ABS), Oceanic Strike Shashoujian(OSS) or Land Battle Shashoujian (LBS).

Directed Energy Weapons

What started as Science Fiction, The Star Wars concept of Ronald Reagan's Strategic Defence Initiative - considered financially unviable then-has come of age today as directed energy weapons (DEW). The directed energy systems can take the form of lasers, high-power microwaves, and electromagnetic pulse weapons. The two most important Chinese organizations involved in R&D of DEW are the Academy of Sciences and the Commissions of Science, Technology and Industry for National Defence (COSTIND).

Laser

Laser, or light amplification with stimulated emission of radiation, has come a long way since its discovery. It has created options for military technology experts to develop a plethora of weapons based on use of lasers. Thus, PLA military experts consider that laser would be useful not only for shooting down aircraft, cruise missiles, PGMs and ballistic missiles but can also be used as an anti-satellite (ASAT) weapon. Laser weapons could also be employed to arm an assortment of platforms including UAVs and satellites. Hence, Laser weapons can be operationalised as SBS, ABS, OSS and LBS.

Lasers can be produced by a number of different methods, ranging from rods of chemically laced glass, to energetic chemical reactions, to the wiggling of free electrons. Beams could either be continuous or short-pulsed or produce intense levels of energy in every wavelength of the electromagnetic spectrum, ranging from infrared to ultraviolet. These characteristics of laser give number of options to weapon designers.

Compared with conventional weapons, which rely on the kinetic or chemical energy of an intercept vehicle, lasers can hit a target with sub-atomic particles or electromagnetic waves. Today, laser beams are capable of destroying targets over great distances. The power output necessary for a laser to reach weapons grade power for ballistic missile defence is a minimum of 1 megawatt (1000 kilowatts).[1] During the past two decades, this technology has advanced considerably in areas such as power, beam control, and pointing and tracking techniques which enables the system to hit a target at great ranges.[2] This energy can be used to engage satellites, aircraft and vehicles, and even has the ability to destroy missiles traveling at supersonic speeds. In addition to being able to engage rapidly moving targets, lasers can be re-directed by mirrors to hit these targets that fall outside line-of-sight range. All this can be done without compromising much of the beam's initial power.[3]

China has developed military lasers for a range of applications, from weapons to radar and from lasing equipment to communications. The US Department of Defence PLA Report 2002 stated that China reportedly is focusing its laser weapon development on antipersonnel, counter precision guided munitions, air defence, and ASAT roles. Use of laser as an Assassin's Mace is visualized by China at different phases of operations. Laser as an ASAT could disrupt US planning, decision making, command and control network systems.

Amongst the LBS, the ZM-87 Portable Laser Distributer (PLD) is the electro-optic countermeasure neodymium laser device. The ZM-87 PLD was primarily intended to blind humans but is also reported to damage photo-electric elements in laser rangefinders, video cameras and missile seekers.[4] Its portability, ease and versatility of operations makes its employment as LBS extremely effective. Two US Navy Helicopters were illuminated by the North Koreans using Chinese made ZM 87 anti-personnel Lasers[5] indicating that the PLD has been operationalised.

The main battle tanks Type 98 LBS, JD-3 integrated laser range finder/ warning/ self-defence device uses a high-powered laser to directly attack the enemy weapon's optics and gunner.[6] The LBS system includes laser warning receiver that warns the crew when their tank is being lased by an enemy laser range finder or by the weapon guidance laser. The turret of the tank is traversed to face the direction of the enemy threat and the laser self defence weapon is activated. Laser self defence weapon then engages the source, the enemy laser. The weapons system works two levels of power. First, the laser weapon uses a low-powered beam for location of the optical system of the enemy weapon. Once located, the power level of the laser is immediately increased. Enhanced laser disables the guidance optics of the enemy weapon and damages the eyesight of the enemy gunner. Once JD3 laser device operability is enhanced, it can be used for communications between friendly tanks[7] and can be elevated to a higher angle than the tank's main gun, making engagement of attack helicopters a possibility. Hence, the laser could then be used as an effective anti-aircraft tool also.

Yet another LBS that China is developing is laser radar or "Ladar". This LBS can illuminate targets in most weather and adverse conditions,[8] thereby enhancing operational effectiveness of the forces. China's attack Ladar has break-through technologies in laser materials, laser radiation materials, imaging spectrum, fast-track positioning control, reversible conversion of high density energy carrier material and laser imaging technology.[9] PLA Army has developed a Ladar system small enough to be placed on an armoured personnel carrier.[10] The target images obtained can be enhanced by technologies inbuilt in a Ladar system by stabilization of images, and by frame averaging to produce a reasonably clear target image.

Yet another laser Shashoujian PLA has developed is a "laser cannon" for tactical missions. In 2009, the PLA tested laser cannon, mounted on a Dahua-class ship[11] against a rocket attack. Thus, a laser cannon can now be mounted on board PLA surface combat vessels, as an anti-aircraft, anti-missiles and anti-satellite measure.[12] It is reported that China has developed a super-power solid-state laser that can launch a laser beam of energy density of 35K joules per square centimeter, for an effective attack range of over 30,000 km. This opens a wide arena for effective operational engagement of adversary hardware.[13]

It is reported that China has sensitive laser technology enabling them to test miniature nuclear weapons and to assist the Chinese Navy in locating US nuclear submarines.

In a defence website it has been reported that on the 50th Anniversary of the PLA Air Force, 2009, a wall mural was created showing a four-turbofan powered transport aircraft using a nose mounted laser attacking a satellite. It was stated that Xi'an Aircraft Company is apparently developing a four-turbofan engine transport aircraft that could carry a chemical laser system and would serve as the test-bed for the Chinese airborne laser weapon prototype similar to American YAL-1.[14] A Chinese military web site suggested that basing a laser on the Moon might overcome the atmospheric distortion Earth-based lasers face in attacking enemy satellites indicating Chinese desire for use of laser as SBS.[15]

Hong Kong Standard has reported that the Chinese have developed a laser-based anti-missile and anti-satellite system. China's system shoots a laser beam that destroys the guidance system and causes the projectile to fall harmlessly to the ground. In addition to hard-kill capabilities, China has the capability to use soft-kill measures to neutralize adversary's space assets and is developing directed energy ASATs, including high-powered microwave and particle beam weapons. In 2006 the Director of the National Reconnaissance Office, Donald Kerr, substantiated reports that China used a ground-based laser to dazzle a US spy satellite over its territory.[16] Reports indicate that China has already tested and deployed a ground-based ASAT laser that can target assets in LEO.[17]

China is inclined to develop inertial confinement nuclear fusion laser. The laser generator technology will assist PLA in developing high-energy laser for anti-ballistic missiles and anti-satellite technology. Shenguang 3 High-Energy Research Center in Mianyang, Sichuan Province, being developed by China Academy of Engineering Physics will enable development of China's next generation of thermonuclear weapons and laser weapons.[18]

Electro Magnetic Pulse

Electro Magnetic Pulse (EMP) is considered as an important war tool by the Chinese due to its versatility for use as Shashoujian. These weapons can be used for degrading or destroying microcircuits, computers, radar and other sensors, communications networks and other electronic systems which form the components of most military ware today. The strong magnetic field and electromagnetic pulse caused by an explosion of these weapons destroys the integrated circuits, interconnects between circuits and components, chips etc and thus paralyzes the radar and communications system[19]. The EMP weapons can be used over land or sea. Once fired against a CBG it can degrade / destroy the functioning of communication and non-communication equipment on board the aircraft carrier and in the vessels around it as well as the ship-mounted missiles and aircraft embarked.[20] EMP attacks can be Nuclear EMP attacks (NEMP) or Nonnuclear EMP (NNEMP) attacks.

(a) **Nuclear Electromagnetic Pulse.** NEMP is a sudden pulse of electromagnetic radiation from a nuclear explosion. The resulting electric fields and magnetic fields interact with electrical/electronic systems to produce a strong and destructive current and voltage surges. High-altitude electromagnetic pulse (HEMP) device is a nuclear warhead detonated hundreds of kilometers above the Earth's surface. HEMP produces the EMP as its main destruction component. The demolition of the nuclear device produces gamma rays which are converted into EMP in the mid-stratosphere. The HEMP explosion result is rapidly changing electrical and magnetic fields which damages electronic and electrical systems within line of sight of the blast but spread over a wide area. NEMP weapons are designed to maximize such effects on electronic systems.[21]

(b) **Non-Nuclear Electromagnetic Pulse.** NNEMP is a weapon-generated electromagnetic pulse without use of nuclear technology. This makes the weapon relatively clean. Wave-shaping circuits and/or microwave generators are added between the pulse source and the antenna of the weapon. This arrangement enables achievement of frequency characteristics of the pulse needed for optimal coupling into the target. NNEMP generators can be carried as a payload of bombs, cruise missiles and drones. The range of NNEMP weapons is lesser than NEMP.[22]

Nuclear and thermonuclear explosions create a large EMP effect that can cause electronic equipment to be overloaded and damaged due to surges in current and voltages. Large nuclear EMP can cause electronic systems within hundreds to over a thousand kilometers of ground zero to be destroyed. The effective power of a NNEMP burst is several million times greater than those of current jammers (reaching 10,000 MW) and can burn unprotected electronic equipment systems as well as destroy the normal operation of computer systems. There is also evidence that China is developing, or has already developed, super-EMP nuclear weapons that generate extraordinarily powerful EMP fields, based partly on design information stolen from the US.[23]

An EMP attack can either come from an intercontinental ballistic missile (LBS); a submarine-launched ballistic missile (OSS); a long-range cruise missile or an orbiting satellite (SBS) armed with a nuclear or non-nuclear EMP warhead. A nuclear burst of one (or more) megaton affects an area of 1600 km radius around it with electro-magnetic pulse in less than one second. Range of EMP at various burst heights effect on India is shown in Figure 2 below.[24]

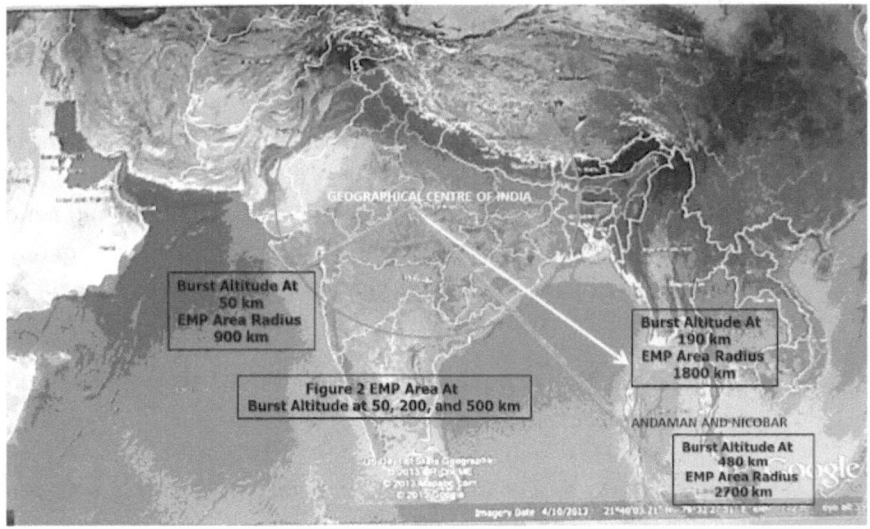

Figure 2:   Range of EMP at various burst heights

An EMP attack will damage all electrical grids over the country where the blast has taken place. It will disable computers and other similar electronic devices with microchips. Most businesses, banking sector and industries will shut down and the entire economy will practically grind to a halt. The effect of EMP is so severe that Satellites within line of sight of the EMP burst will also be damaged, which would adversely affect military command, control, communications, computers, intelligence, surveillance and reconnaissance (C^4ISR). Land-based intercontinental ballistic missiles will be rendered unserviceable in their silos. Anti-ballistic missile defences will suffer the same fate.[25] As the Ballistic Missile Defence is rendered ineffective, the vulnerability to conventional attacks gets greatly enhanced.

Richard Fisher, a China military analyst, said EMP warheads are likely to be an option for China's new DF-21D anti-ship ballistic missile for the purpose of attacking large US Navy ships without inflicting immediate massive casualties.[26] A missile that uses a burst of RF energy to disable an incoming missile or aircraft and has "radio-flash" HPM bomb is being developed by PLA for its Air Force.[27]

American Websites have expressed concerns that China's military is developing electromagnetic pulse weapons that Beijing plans to use against US aircraft carriers in any future conflict over Taiwan. It has been reported that China's high-altitude EMP capability could be used in two different ways:-

(a) As a surprise measure after China's initial strike against Taiwan and aircraft carrier strike group assets.

(b) As a bluff intended to dissuade the US from defending Taiwan with carrier strike groups.[28]

Use of EMP over India can leave the Nation electronically blind. A strike in IOR can severely degrade Indian fleets afloat including the CBG. However, the EMP attack over India would need to be properly calibrated in terms of power, height of burst and point of burst so as to not affect neighbouring countries.

High Power Microwave Weapons

High Power Microwave (HPM) is yet another technology in use for Shashoujian Weapons. HPM uses electromagnetic wave with a peak power between 100MW-100GW and operating frequency lying between 1-300 GHz for generation of EMP. Strong EM pulse generated by HPM weapons can damage equipment, cause people to temporarily lose their operating abilities, or even kill them. These pulses can propagate through clouds, dust, rain and even kill personnel in an enclosed space like an armoured vehicle. HPM weapons can be carried on multiple platforms like cruise missile, UAVs, fixed platforms etc. HPM can be researched by computer simulations[29] and thus their development can be kept under wraps, making them a mace that could dazzle in war. The potential of HPM for use as LBS, ABS, SBS and ability to evolve HPM using computer simulators makes this technology extremely attractive for use as Assassin's Mace weaponry.

HPM weapons have the potential to produce the same effect as EMP but without a nuclear explosion and its undesirable side effects.[30] HPM can produce a narrower powerful beam of energy.[31] Many counter-EMP measures do not work for HPM devices. Miniaturized HPM weapons can fit in an artillery shell or missile warhead and can combine the functions of a radar and weapon, and facilitate targeting by increasing power output as it approaches its target.[32]

How could these weapons be employed operationally? These Microwave weapons can be used to shut down enemy radar, communications, computers and other electronics in an opening salvo making the adversary blind, disorganized and cause disorientation. Then the weapons could jam electronics of attacking aircraft and anti-radiation missiles, thereby taking the sting out from enemy's attack. Simultaneously, HPM could be used as an ASAT weapons which could inflict long term damage to navigation, control, communication and early warning capabilities of the enemy. It is reported that the PLA has deployed a HPM warhead on its latest version of DF – 15 SRBM[33], and has a "radio-flash" HPM bomb for use by the PLAAF [34]. Such technologies once developed can be used for space-based weapons to attack satellites and missiles.[35] It would not be incorrect to presume that China is looking at HPM war head for longer range missiles and satellites.

Latest research in HPM weapons is on the concept of multi-pulse repeating HPM transmitting device that can repeatedly strike the same target or attack a new target. The multi-pulse repeating HPM transmitting device can be used on reusable cruise missile. HPM RF beaming system which burn the electronics of guided weapons[36] have also been developed. This gives China a cutting edge in battle space both over land and sea.

Unmanned Combat Platforms

PLA has been investing heavily in a new generation of Unmanned Combat Platforms (UCP) to counter the threats posed by manned combat aircraft, ships, as well as land forces. UCP are unmanned, highly maneuverable platforms capable of replacing manned platforms on high-risk missions. Thus, UCP vehicles are another military "transformation" technology being pursued by the PLA for air, land and underwater missions. Hence, UCPs can be classified under categories LBS, OSS, and ABS. The UCP are likely to be used for intelligence tasks, electronic warfare, targeting and unmanned combat engagements and could also launch suicidal missions. These platforms are important for Chinese A2/AD operations. The versatility, variety and flexibility of UCP make them important Shashoujian weapons.

PLA is reported to be developing a range of airborne unmanned aircraft (UAV, UCAV), unmanned ship and underwater vehicles (USV, UUV), and unmanned ground combat vehicles.[37] Initial PLA versions were made similar to US 1960s Firebee drone captured in the Vietnam War, but there-after evolved in its programs with South Africa and Russia UAV and UCAV technologies. PLA has converted about 200 older J-6 fighters to serve as UCAVs. At successive Zhuhai air shows since 1996, the PLA has unveiled progressively more sophisticated UAVs and UCAVs. China has also tested an unmanned submarine able to descend to a depth of 6,000 meters,[38] an OSS with significant capabilities. At the Beijing Military Museum, on PLA Eightieth Anniversary, the PLA revealed a new tracked combat robot similar to several models used by the US and European armed forces. The PLA's tracked vehicle was equipped to climb stairs and had two weapon stations.[39]

In 2006, China unveiled a concept turbofan-powered surveillance UAV of the size and shape of Global Hawk surveillance UAV and box-wing Soar Dragon turbo-fan powered surveillance UAV. The Shenyang Aircraft Corporation unveiled its concept supersonic Dark Sword UCAV.[40] Lijian "Sharp Sword" UCAV is said to have a wingspan of 14 meters and is powered by a single jet WP7 engine with ordnance payload not exceeding 2,000 kgs. The Chinese CM-506 small-diameter bomb with a range of 130 km (80 miles) against land or maritime targets, showcased at Air Show China 2012, is one of the weapons being recommended for the Lijian.[41] A number of UAVs like the BZK – 001, BZK – 002, BZK – 005 and BZK – 006 are operational today and PLA today is developing UAV detection capability as part of its air and missile defence infrastructure[42]. Other unmanned vehicles developments include the W-30 and W-50 tactical UAVs like the Searcher, anti-radar drone, ZOND series of UAVs.[43] In April 2012 it was reported that three UAVs practised vertical take-offs and landings on the rear deck of China's Type 054A frigate "Zhoushan". Analysts speculate that the UAVs have good stealth capability and can carry 34 kg for six hours. In yet another progress forward, Wing Loong armed UAV was displayed at China biennial air show in November 2012 and then in Paris Air Show in June 2013. China is now negotiating to sell armed UAVs to Asian and African countries.

New unmanned patrol/surveillance boat useful for long-distance reconnaissance, communication relay, electronic interference, sea monitor, target strike, target damage assessment as well as submarine mine search and anti-submarine combat was also revealed. China has also developed UUV with assistance from Russia.[44] In 2007, Chinese television showed a PLAN minesweeper using a UUV for countermine operations. PRC UUVs under the "863" program have artificial intelligence and automatic control ability to reach depths of 6000 meters and form the basis for unmanned underwater combat vehicles (UUCVs).[45] Chinese UUVs include the Hairen 1 remote controlled undersea robot prototype built in the mid-1980s by the Shenyang Institute of Automation Robotics Laboratory; the Tansuozhe UUV in 1993; and with Russian researchers, the CR-01 UUV based on the Russian MT-88 and Zhishui 3 UUV prototype with dual tail propellers and two cross-tunnel thrusters.[46]

Beijing University of Aeronautics and Astronautics has developed the SPC-3 Robo-fish UUV prototype. Other projects include glider-type UUVs designed by Tianjin University. Chinese Navy is conducting research in UUV swarming techniques and is developing UUVs as nodes for larger information networks. In the "swarm concept" UUVs form a part of an undersea network, where some are optimized for sensing, others for shooting and still others function as communications relay stations. These would act like communication buoys that might surface occasionally to send a signal to a satellite[47] thereby improving China's ISR and targeting capabilities.

Electromagnetic Weapons

Electromagnetic Weapons are a game changing armament and will not only enhance ranges of engagement but will also enhance fire assaults effectiveness by increase in fire density at target end. The Shashoujian use magnets, or a combination of magnets and chemical propellants, to give projectiles speed and range far greater than is possible with chemical propellants alone. Electromagnetic weapons have the potential to increase fire rates to artillery-size projectiles along with the range and speed of a short-range ballistic missile, and thus they can be used for missile defence as well as strike missions.[48] The fire assault, fire density and fire support ranges significantly improve by use of these weapons. Commanders in field thus have greater flexibility and options for employment of his forces. The PLA is known to have a great interest in electromagnetic guns and is researching several systems, including electromagnetic guns and combined chemical and electromagnetic ("electro-thermal") guns[49]. In 1996 PRC analyst Ch'en Huan noted that electromagnetic guns would be useful for space warfare. Hence, use of electromagnetic weapons as potential SBS by China cannot be ignored.

As ground based Shashoujian (LBS), EM weapons application can be for both offensive and defensive purposes. China is reportedly developing electromagnetic plate armor. These armor plates can be electromagnetically fired into oncoming shells or missiles to protect armored vehicles-a protective/defensive role.[50] With electromagnetic guns it is possible to give artillery shells the range and speed of a tactical ballistic missile, allowing thousands of long-range artillery rounds to supplement hundreds of missiles[51]. This would enable continuous engagement of enemy troops in the battle field at extremely low operating costs.

An unconfirmed report emerged in January 2008 that the PLA had tested a 25 kg rail gun round in 2006 and was able to deploy a 50 kg round with a range over 200nm. In early 2011, a picture of Chinese small-caliber rail gun was posted on a Chinese web page. However, it is not known whether this represented an actual test model or was an engineering model for display purposes. PLA's rail gun deployments can affect offensive and defensive operations.[52] It will force China's adversaries to rethink current strategies of combat. These weapons add a new paradigm to war-fighting.

Information Warfare

> *Information war is a crucial stage of high-tech war. . . . At its heart are information technologies, fusing intelligence war, strategic war, electronic war, guided missile war, a war of "motorization", a war of firepower—a total war. It is a new type of warfare.*
>
> *—Major General Wang Pufeng*
> *(Father of Chinese IW)*[53]

Chinese strategists believe that the US military's might is dependent to a great degree on its effective integration and use of information technology as these not only provide advance intelligence information but also enable command, control, communication, decision making and direction of military assets. China considers that more than the capabilities of individual platforms, such as fighters or aircraft carriers, it is its C^4ISR[54]

system that gives the US an edge over other countries. US forces' heavy dependence on the C⁴ISR System is thus considered by PLA as a major US military vulnerability. The C⁴ISR System is thus considered a COG, a prime target for engagement.[55]

China had been modernizing the PLA in the context of 'local war under conditions of informationization', while focused on strategic areas of space, nuclear and information warfare, with 'Informationization' being placed at the core. China considers these as Assassin's Mace weaponry. PLA's advancements in Information Technology capabilities has acted as a catalyst in acquiring integrated IW capability which aims to interfere with the adversaries' networks while protecting own networks and systems. Computer network operations (CNO)[56] and Electronic Warfare attack on the adversaries' C⁴ISR networks and other key information assets assist in information dominance. IW is defined as the comprehensive use, with intelligence support, of military deception, operational secrecy, psychological warfare, electronic warfare, and substantive destruction to assault the enemy's whole information system including personnel; and to disrupt the enemy's information flow, in order to impact, weaken, and destroy the enemy's command and control capability, while keeping one's own command and control capability from being affected by similar enemy actions.[57] One of the main roles of IW is to create windows of opportunity for forces to operate without detection or with a reduced risk of counter attack by exploiting the periods of blindness, deafness or paralysis created by information attacks.

At the strategic and campaign level one of the key goals for the PLA is Information dominance[58]. PLA integrates CNO strikes on the enemy's command and control architecture with hard kill using missiles, airstrikes or Special Forces. A preemptive Computer Network strike in a time phased approach would maximize adversary's combat capability degradation. The operations could begin weeks/days before the actual hostilities to facilitate injection and/or activation of data collection software for intelligence gathering, insertion of malware for destructive missions. Closer to the actual combat, PLA could begin modification and corruption of the data to deceive the adversary or confuse him to such an extent that his operational planning would go astray.

The asymmetric nature of cyber warfare has accordingly found favour with PLA as it is very difficult to identify any battle indicators of offensive operations planned or underway. The resources required to launch a cyber offensive are few and with the technologies available today, it is easy to, create an appropriate cyber weapon to target networks - exploit it or damage it. Even the attribution of a cyber-attack is extremely difficult. Cyber operations are undetectable prior to launch and once the attack has occurred, it could be extremely difficult to determine its origin. Another advantage in cyber space is the time taken to execute operational intent. Cyber-attacks happen at the speed of light, leaving the adversary hardly any time to react. The initial strike could eliminate effective defence, render counter attack ineffective and strike much faster than any possible human response.

Cyber weapons, in essence, are a 'one-use-only' kind of weapons and their mere existence is a closely guarded secret. It is very hard for the adversary to defend against a weapon which has neither been seen in action nor is one aware of the vulnerability it is intended to exploit. The life span of cyber weapons is limited as its design. The cyber weapon in its life span is focused on a particular vulnerability which it intends to exploit.[59]. Once the vulnerability is 'patched' the cyber weapon becomes ineffective, at least against that system. Cyber weapons and Cyber-attacks need not necessarily target a military objective. Cyber-attacks are at low costs, secrecy can be maintained, attribution of an attack is difficult while the effect on adversary networks is extremely damaging. It is thus not difficult to understand why China is pursuing information technologies with such zeal.

Space Warfare

The PLA is rapidly improving its space and counter-space capabilities in order to advance CCP interests and defend against perceived challenges to sovereignty and territorial integrity. Space capabilities not only enable PLA to conduct military operations at increasingly greater distances from Chinese shores by assisting in early warning and vectoring assets to required area but also enable integrated air and space picture and survivable communication architecture.[60] China uses two types of satellites for secure military communication, the Fenghuo series, for secure tactical level communication using C-band and UHF, and the Shentong geostationary satellites series, for secured voice and data communications services for ground users using Ku-band. In May, 2012 China launched the Chinasat-

2A which will enhance the PLA's voice and data usage capabilities as it gets informationalised.[61]

The PLA has been developing ASAT weapons as a national priority since at least the early 1990s. China demonstrated an ability to engage targets in space as part of a broader effort to field a national aerospace security system. China links counter-space with an ability to track and engage all flight vehicles transiting space, including ballistic missiles. China's counter-space program is expected to be in place by 2025. Historically, in 2004, the PLA began a series of three direct ascent ASAT tests. The successful fourth test destroyed the FY-1C weather satellite in January 2007. China's direct-ascent, kinetic-kill ASAT launch is a variant of the Chinese Kaituozhe-1 developed by the China Aerospace Science and Industry Corporation (CASIC). The launch vehicle's guidance package was aided by ground based radars. ASAT's kinetic-kill vehicle (KKV) was a modified HQ-19 warhead. Aside from the direct-ascent KKV China has successfully tested, it is also possible that direct-ascent ASATs could be armed with the EMP (nuclear or non-nuclear) warheads. China's successful tests of a KKV in January 2007 and January 2010 demonstrate an ability to intercept polar orbiting satellites and rudimentary medium range ballistic missiles during the mid-course of flight.[62]

In January 2013, China launched three small maneuvering satellites as part of its ASAT program, including one with a robotic arm that can be used to capture or destroy orbiting satellites. In May 13, 2013, China fired a missile into space from the Xichang Satellite Launch Center in Western China on a ballistic trajectory to nearly geosynchronous Earth orbit and was intended to test the launch vehicle component of a new high-altitude ASAT capability. This signals China's intent to develop an ASAT capability to target satellites in an altitude range that includes Global Positioning System (GPS) and other military and intelligence satellites. In September 2013, China launched a satellite into space carried on a missile called the "Kuaizhou,". The launch served to test a new solid-fueled launch vehicle, a capability that would allow PLA to quickly replace satellites that might be damaged or destroyed in an ASAT with small and capable satellites. China's microsatellites have many potential offensive uses such as maneuvering in range of an adversary's satellite and either latching on as "parasitic microsat" to disrupt proper functions, or merely exploding within range of a target satellite to destroy it.[63]

General William Shelton, Commander USAF, Space Command has stated that China currently has a missile that can destroy US satellites and that strategic military satellite are vulnerable to attack in a future space war. Pentagon is considering a major shift to smaller satellites.

China is reported to be developing a submarine launch vehicle for ASAT operations.[64]

China has also implemented the Beidou Navigation System, an independently established and operated system that provides accurate, reliable all-time, all-weather positioning, navigation and timing services[65]. In December 2012, China's Beidou regional satellite navigation system became fully operational and available for commercial use using 16 satellites and a network of ground stations. Beidou provides subscribers in Asia with 24-hour precision, navigation, and timing services, as well as the ability to send and receive text messages up to 120 Chinese characters. China plans to expand Beidou into a global satellite navigation system by 2020.[66] According to Jane's, by 2020, Beidou 2 envisions a full-scale system of at least five geostationary and 30 non-geostationary satellites providing a global coverage in two modes: free "open" services available to commercial customers with 10-metre location-tracking accuracy, and restricted "authorised" services providing positioning, velocity and timing communications estimated at 10 centimeter accuracy for the Chinese government and military.

Thermobaric Weapons

Yet another LBS and ABS high end technology weapons developed by China are the Thermobaric Weapons. Thermobaric Weapons destroy target by generating heat and pressure in a short time and with tremendous impact. Thermobaric strength lies in the ability to create a destructive effect far in excess of conventional high explosives of the same size. Fuel-air explosives (FAEs) are one type of thermobaric weapon. FAEs are usually missile warheads or bombs that create a cloud of atomized fuel, which is then ignited to create a great amount of heat and pressure.[67]

Russia is known to have provided at least one type of thermobaric weapon to the PLA and has provided additional technology. China has FAE bombs for aircraft and is at least researching missile warhead FAEs for short and medium range missiles. The PLA is co-producing a

Russian-designed personal thermobaric weapon similar to SHMEL, the Bumblebee, RPO-A, the Russian Make. SHMEL has a shoulder-launched rocket loaded with an aerosol warhead which creates a fuel cloud at the target end which is later ignited by second explosive. It is useful against buildings, pill boxes and reinforced bunkers. SHMEL has the range of about 300 meters and packs the destructive power of a 122mm artillery shell and can cause total destruction when fired into a medium-sized house or an earthen bunker. SHMEL was used by Russian forces in Chechnya.

Russia is now marketing thermobaric warheads for its guided anti-tank missiles, which may also interest the PLA. Russian KAB-1500 that PLA purchased in 2002 also comes in a version equipped with a thermobaric warhead.[68] In 2007 China revealed a thermobaric round which can be fired from a RPG[69], raising a possibility of it being co-produced with Iran or Pakistan. This has serious implications for India.

PLA Hypersonic Vehicle

Hypersonic strike aircraft is a transformational weapon. Hypersonic aerospace flight vehicles merge the air and space domains together in an operational perspective. Aerospace strike systems are launched into a sub-orbital trajectory in near space by a ballistic missile or by strike system that utilizes an air breathing supersonic combustion ramjet (scramjet)[70] engine to propel a vehicle to hypersonic speeds.[71] Key technological areas include high lift-to-drag ratio delivery vehicles, high temperature materials for thermal protection, precision navigation, guidance and control, and ability to maintain external radio frequency links through plasma in near space.

Vehicle design relies on conventional ballistic missile technology for ascent into a sub-orbital trajectory. The missile then releases the post-boost vehicle to glide and maneuver toward the intended target.[72] Aerodynamically configured to glide toward its target, the flight vehicle adopts hybrid characteristics of both ballistic and cruise missiles. In its initial stage of flight, sources indicate the flight vehicle would reach hypersonic speeds between Mach 8 and Mach 12.[73]

These aircraft can serve as low earth orbit launch vehicles and be the successor to the strategic bomber and ICBM.[74] Built on technology developed for the Space Shuttle and the single-stage-to-orbit test vehicle, a hypersonic strike vehicle can be as fast as an ICBM, but could also be recalled if necessary to strike again. It could deliver non-nuclear warheads accurately whose destructive impact would be compounded due to their hypersonic speed. Their speed and range would obviate the need for overseas bases[75] an important consideration as warfare is now global.

PLA is developing hypersonic strike vehicles with zeal. China built a Hypersonic Propulsion Test Facility in Beijing featuring a wind tunnel that can generate velocities up to Mach 5.6.[76] Access to Russian technology provided PLA opportunity to build its own hypersonic research and development capability. China's interest and efforts to develop hypersonic strike vehicles have been continuous and focused as per chronology below:-

(a) At the 1997 Moscow Air Show, Vice Chairman General Liu Huaqing views the Russian Raduga hypersonic test engine designed for speeds up to Mach 6.5.[77]

(b) In early 2001 China negotiated to contribute to a novel hypersonic suborbital program of the Leninets Holding Company called Ayaks. The program was on kerosene-fueled "magneto-plasmo-chemical" engine that would allow the vehicle to travel from Russia to the United States in 1.6 hours.[78]

(c) A French report suggested that China had tested a scramjet-powered hypersonic test vehicle in late 2006.[79]

(d) In December 2007, Chinese Internet imagery appeared to show a model of a possible hypersonic test vehicle, having a missile shape with long tapered delta wings.[80]

(e) May 2012, testing of hypersonic wind tunnel.[81]

(f) January 2014, first test flight of new hypersonic guide vehicle.[82]

The PLA is also focused on achieving technology breakthroughs to enable advanced supersonic (up to Mach 4) and hypersonic (Mach 5 and higher) combat. The 1986 "869 Program" to select a manned space vehicle gave a boost to university and corporate level hypersonic research. Today the Chengdu and Shenyang Aircraft Corporations have multiple hypersonic programs underway, while the China Aerospace Corporation works on a Shuttle-like space plane. Major Chinese university centers for

PLA funded or directed hypersonic research in aerodynamics, materials and engines These include the Institute of Mechanics, Chinese Academy of Sciences; Northwestern Polytechnic University; Harbin Institute of Technology; National University of Defence Technology; Beijing University; the Beijing University of Aeronautics and Astronautics; the Nanjing University of Aeronautics and Astronautics and the Nanjing University of Science and Technology.

A mid-2010 study by researchers at the Institute of Mechanics brought out PLA interest in a Mach 3 speed lifting body platform as near time objective. Experts believe that unmanned or manned version of sufficient size could conduct surveillance or strike missions at very high altitudes and could affect current US interception capabilities.[83] In May 2012, the China Academy of Sciences announced successful acceptance testing of its new super-large JF12 hypersonic wind tunnel (reportedly the largest in the world), capable of replicating flying conditions at Mach 5 to 9. This project was one of eight of China's National Mid-and-Long-Term Scientific and Technological Development Outline Plan (2006-2020). [84]

China's military conducted the first flight test of a new hypersonic vehicle in January 14 capable of delivering warheads through US missile defences. The hypersonic vehicle is a major step in China's secretive strategic nuclear and conventional military and missile programs. The new hypersonic vehicle was detected traveling at extremely high speeds during the flight test over China. The hypersonic craft appears designed to be launched atop one of China's intercontinental ballistic missiles, and then glide and maneuver at speeds of up to 10 times the speed of sound from near space en route to its target.[85] China is engaged in two hypersonic flight vehicle programs, a post-boost vehicle designed to launch from a missile, and scramjet-powered vehicle that can take off independently or be launched from a bomber.[86]

China favours pre-emptive strike as an option and advocates gradual escalation of conflict, with the view to break a Nations will to fight by inflicting damaging strikes. The hypervelocity vehicle development supports Chinese design of battle. Not only will it be an effective pre-emptive weapon but will also address the requirement of quick and damaging strikes to compel early closure of battle in terms favourable to China.[87]

The military advantages of hypersonic craft include precise targeting, very rapid delivery of weapons, and greater survivability against missile and space defences.

Nano Technology

Micro-machines and robots are a key RMA technology that will enable new small weapons, such as 25-pound "nano" satellites, palm-sized reconnaissance aircraft, or small robot vehicles that could replace guard-dogs and sentries. At the Zhuhai show, a Chinese company stated their intention to build new "nano" satellites, which experts believe could be used for anti satellite missions. China has revealed a new 20-millimeter-sized helicopter, which could form the basis for a micro-reconnaissance vehicle.[88] In addition, China has also revealed research to produce intelligent human-sized robots that could also in the future help produce robot soldiers.[89] PLA considers Nanotechnology as key transformational military technology and hence China is investing in Nano-Technology to develop SBS and LBS.

It has been reported that China has at least 100 nanotechnology related programs underway employing 3,000 engineers and scientists. A 2006 Chinese article lists seven military applications for nanotechnology as given below[90]:-

(a) Nano-discs, with storage capacities manifolds that of current computers

(b) Nano-tube structures, that are hundred times stronger than steel

(c) Genetic weapons that can target specific genetic features.

(d) Super-thin stealth radar-absorbing coatings for weapon platforms.

(e) Micro-weapons.

(f) Nano-satellites.

(g) Soldier equipment such as armor cloth and laser-protection head gear.

This extreme versatility of Nano-technology leads to varied usage in warfare. It can be used as SBS, ABS, LBS, OSS as well as part of information warfare. Nano army enables improvements reconnaissance and counter-reconnaissance, stealth and counter-stealth and sabotage and counter-sabotage. Nano operational concepts that would enhance the shock and awe effects in future battle field could be stealth surprise attack operations, micro vital point operations, concealed paralysis operations and nano-deterrence operations.[91]

Major General Sun Bailin of the Academy of Military Science in an article "Nanotechnology weapons on future battlefields" in National Defence, June 15, 1996 has stated that the MEMS (micro-elctro-mechanical systems) revolution will usher in a 'nano-era' in the 21st century encompassing; nano-biology, nano-manufacturing, nano-mechanics, nano-electronics, nano-micrology, nano-control, nano-surveying and the study of nano-materials. Major General Sun Bailin suggested that in the future US military equipment would be vulnerable to attack by armies of sound-energy-powered "ant robots." 863 Program also featured mini robots for internal medical inspection of humans.[92]

Some technological areas where Nano inroads are being made are[93]:-

(a) 'Ant robots' which could replicate themselves and lie dormant in enemy war equipment till activated to destroy them. Blood vessel submarines for molecular surgery can be used during medical treatment in peace and war.[94]

(b) 'Distributed Battlefield Micro scale Sensor Networks', dispersing swarms of these molecular devices, which are practically invisible, for gathering battlefield environment information.

(c) 'Nano-satellites' information gathering molecular devices that could form a local distributed satellite system. For complete 24/7 earth coverage a total of 648 nano-satellites could be placed in orbit (with 36 nano-satellites placed evenly into each of 18 equally spaced solar stationary orbits).

(d) Blood vessel submarines for molecular surgery.

Crucial military technology of the 21st century would be nanotechnology and nano-weapons that would cause fundamental changes in military thought and affairs.[95] Nano-materials development is the main objective for the near future. The development of bio-nano-technology and nano-medical technology would be an objective for the medium term, whereas the development of nano-electronics and nano-chips can be a long-term objective. Nano-tech Shashoujian thus brings a new paradigm to war fighting.

Biotechnical Weapons

Biotechnology is the use of living systems and organisms to develop or make useful products, or "any technological application that uses biological systems, living organisms or derivatives thereof, to make or modify products or processes for specific use" (UN Convention on Biological Diversity, Art. 2). Depending on the tools and applications, it often overlaps with the related fields of bioengineering and biomedical engineering.[96] Bio technology is yet another area of work of the 863 Program. PLA is conducting research on the military applications of this class of technologies.

Bio-electronic equipment, biological bombs, bio-navigation, bio-energy and bionic power are some of the areas of interest.[97] The Chinese writers identified several possible military biotechnical applications. Bio-electronic equipment such as protein-based computers would have more than hundred million times higher capacities than existing computers and would be immune to electromagnetic weapons.[98] They are more difficult to detect compared to programs that are developing nuclear weapons.[99]

A biological weapon, a two component system, has one portion to host bacteria and the other, virulent plasmid, and the two are mixed before deploying.[100] Biological bombs could be nearly six times more powerful than conventional explosives. Bio-navigation could be applied to micro-weapons to enhance their accuracy. Bio-energy sources could use chemicals to produce hydrogen, which when combined with small amounts of petroleum fuel will power weapons to longer ranges. Bionic power could replicate the strength of human muscles. Bioengineering could be used to create fighting animal soldiers or even artificial people making biotechnology products a combat disruptive technology.[101]

China's military big step toward fielding the bionic soldiers is an exoskeleton suit that multiplies normal muscle strength. Designed by the General Hospital for the Nanjing Military Region gives ordinary soldiers the strength to carry 36 kilogram boxes as easily as an ordinary backpack.

The bionic suits worn outside clothing reduce the pressure exerted by heavy loads on a soldier's skeletal system by 50%. The aim is to augment the physical strength of PLA troops and enabling them to carry machinery, tools and even munitions. The ultimate goal is to enhance all the physical capabilities of soldiers, letting them run faster, jump higher and hit harder, according to a Dr Zhou, Nanjing hospital.[102]

Stealth and Counter-stealth

The radar evading stealth and counter-stealth technologies are critical for future warfare. These technologies enable undetected penetration of weapon platforms in adversary area and prevent enemy war fighting equipment catching China's military unaware. It could be LBS, ABS or OSS.

At the 1998 Zhuhai Air Show the Chinese company 'Seek Optics' revealed its work on coatings designed to deflect radar energy, and on computer programs for aiding the design of stealthy objects. By using imported supercomputers and commercial finite element analysis software, the PRC is believed to be able to calculate the radar reflectivity of shaped objects. There are also reports that China may apply stealth coatings to improve the penetrating capability of combat aircraft like the Xian JH-7 strike fighter. Stealth coatings will also likely be used to improve the capabilities of future land-attack cruise missiles. Stealth fighter J-20 is designed to engage enemy fighters at high altitude while the stealth fighter J-31 is likely to be used in operations against ground targets at medium or low altitude.[103]

PLA has demonstrated its ability to apply stealth technology to naval warship design the No. 168 and No. 170 class air defence destroyers and Type 054 frigate. Today PLA has several types of Metric-Wave radar and even employs one on its No. 170 class destroyer and other platforms. When combined with modern computers, metric-wave technology has great counter-stealth potential.[104] J-231 metric-wave radar has high anti-stealth capability. Metric wave radar technology dates back to the 1930s and uses large-frequency radio wavelengths, whereas most passive stealth technology is designed to counter the far smaller wavelengths of modern radar. When combined with modern computers, metric-wave technology has great counter-stealth potential.[105]

The PLAN's new Luyang guided-missile destroyers, Type 054 guided-missile frigates, and Houbei-class fast attack craft use stealth shaping and stealth coatings. LUYANG III incorporates the PLAN's first multipurpose vertical launch system, capable of launching ASCM, land attack cruise missiles (LACM), surface-to-air missiles (SAM) and anti-submarine rockets.[106] Stealth frigate Number 586 is a new design with sloped surfaces made as clean as possible to reduce superstructure clutter. It features advanced technologies that will make it harder to detect by radar, sonar and infrared methods.[107]

Chinese military technical literature indicates the likelihood of substantial Chinese research regarding stealth materials, stealth-shaping, and stealth for turbofan engines. This literature may also indicate a Chinese interest in "Plasma Stealth" technology in which a field of charged plasma particles (plasma) absorbs radar signals, greatly reducing the requirement for radical stealth shaping for aircraft.[108] China's fifth generation multirole combat aircraft make extensive use of stealth technology.

Supercavitating Underwater Weapons

Supercavitating underwater weapons move through water at very high velocities, sometimes faster than sound. They are able to move quickly as they form an air bubble or cavitation around the structure. Once launched, there is little defence against such high-speed underwater weapons. They are envisioned for use as torpedoes, anti-torpedoes, anti-mines or missiles that travel underwater and then air-launch near the shore to defeat antimissile defences.[109]

Russia is the leader in super cavitation technology and in 1977 fielded the Shkval (Squall) rocket torpedo, which can achieve speeds up to 200 knots, or 100 meters per second through water. Shkval speed far exceeds that of any standard torpedo speed due super cavitation.[110] The torpedo flies in a gas bubble created by outward deflection of water by its specially shaped nose cone and the expansion of gases from its engine. By keeping water from coming into contact with the surface of the body of the torpedo, drag is significantly reduced allowing extremely high speeds.

The missile controls its direction using four fins that skim the inner surface of the super cavitation envelope. To change direction, the fin or fins on the inside of the desired turn are extended and the opposing fins are retracted. To make faster turns, the push plate on the nose can be used to control the shape of the bubble the missile is traveling in.[111] An advanced version of the Shkval is reportedly capable of 300-knot speeds. In August 1998 the PRC was reported to have purchased forty Shkval rocket torpedoes from Kazakhstan. PLA also has programs underway to develop supercavitating underwater weapons using Shkval weapons to aid the development of its own supercavitating weapons. There is speculation that a PLAN officer died while observing the testing of a new version of the Shkval on the Kursk when it sank.[112]

Shkval rocket torpedo weighs 6,000 lbs and travels at 200 knots and has a range of 7,500 yards. It is guided by autopilot and with its high speed makes evasive maneuvers by carriers or nuclear submarines difficult. There is no known defence against this Shashoujian which is a submarine and carrier buster.[113]

The Assassin's Mace weapons are game changers of tomorrow's battle due to the asymmetry it brings in. Their effect on Sino-India engagement needs to be studied in detail for India to take suitable counter measures.

Endnotes

1. Kochemes, Alane, Gudgel, The Viability of Directed Energy weapons, The Heritage Foundation, April 2006

2. Ibid

3. Spencer, Jack and Jay Carafono, Use of Directed Energy Weapons to Protect Critical Infra structure, The Heritage Foundation, August 2004

4. http://en.wikipedia.org/wiki/ZM-87

5. Two US Navy Helicopters were illuminated by the North Korean using Chinese made ZM 87 anti-personnel Lasers,(David Crane in www.defencereview.com)

6. Jon Dougherty, China Set to Field World's Most Powerful Tank, December 2003, www.wnd/2003/05/18720/

7. http://www.army-guide.com/eng/product2387.html

8. Richard D Fisher, China's Military Modernisation: Building for Regional and Global Reach, Praeger Security International, 2008

9. Secret Chinese laser weapon, http://www.defence.pk/forums/chinese-defence/110402-secret-chinese-laser-weapon.html

10. Global Security, Foreign Help For Hi-Tech Weapons http://www.globalsecurity.org/military/library/report/2004/04fisher/5hitech.htm

11. A Dahua-class ship has a fully-laden displacement of 6,000 tonnes, a speed of 20 knots and a crew of 80. The ship is designed to test radar and weapons systems for the PLA before they are mounted to regular combat vessels. The country's DH-10 cruise missile, HHQ-9, HHQ-10 air defence missiles and vertical launching system were all tested aboard the ship since 2002

12. PLA Navy to trial ship-mounted laser cannon, http://www.wantchinatimes.com/news-subclass-cnt.aspx?id=20130912000097&cid=1101

13. China's Shauguang 3 Super Laser, constructed by Shauguang Laser Facility has produced 48 laser beam of 200 KJ.

14. PLA's weapons that will blow your mind, http://www.defence.pk/forums/chinese-defence/128697-plas-weapons-will-blow-your-mind.html

15. Richard D Fisher, China's Military Modernisation, Building for Regional and Global Reach, Greenwood Publishing, 2008

16. Satellite Laser ranging In China,www.ucusa.org/nuclear-weapons and global security/space weapons/china-laser-us.html

17. Globalsecurity.org while acknowledging Donald Kerr reports has brought out that Dalian University of Technology design team was awarded top PRC Science and Technology Award in January 2009 for development of ASAT system.

18   Chan Kai Yee, China Developing Mystic Powerful Laser Canon, Hypersonic Aircraft, http://tiananmenstremendousachievements.wordpress.com/2013/09/04/china-developing-mystic-powerful-laser-canon-hypersonic-aircraft/

19   Richard D Fisher, China's Military Modernisation, Building for Regional and Global Reach, Greenwood Publishing, 2008

20   Roger Cliff, MarkBurles, Michael S. Chase, Derek Eaton, Kevin L. Pollpeter, Entering the Dragon's Lair: Chinese Anti-access Strategies and their Implications for the United States , 2007

21   www.en.wikipedia.org

22   ibid

23   Mr. Pry, President of the group EMPact America, as quoted in Report: China building electromagnetic pulse weapons for use against U.S. carriers,http://www.washingtontimes.com/news/2011/jul/21/beijing-develops-radiation-weapons/#ixzz2hJMueXkO

24   EMP coverage has been made on map of Indian sub continent available in Google maps, imagery dated 4/10/2013.

25   China Developing Super Electromagnet Pulse Bomb To Use In War Against U.S., http://www.examiner.com/article/china-developing-super-electromagnet-pulse-bomb-to-use-war-against-u-s

26   Report: China building electromagnetic pulse weapons for use against U.S. carriers,http://www.washingtontimes.com/news/2011/jul/21/beijing-develops-radiation-weapons/#ixzz2hJMueXkO

27   Richard D Fisher, China's Military Modernisation, Building for Regional and Global Reach, Greenwood Publishing, 2008

28   Ibid

29   Guoqi Ni, Benqing Gao, Junwei Lu, Research on High Power Microwave weapons.

30   Richard D Fisher, China's Military Modernisation, Building for Regional and Global Reach, Greenwood Publishing, 2008

31   http://www.washingtonpost.com/blogs/checkpoint-washington/post/us-speculated-on-chinas-use-of-electromagnetic-radiation-on-taiwan/2011/07/21/gIQAyVZNTI_blog.html

32   Richard D Fisher, China's Military Modernisation, Building for Regional and Global Reach, Greenwood Publishing, 2008

33   Ronald O' Rourke, China Naval Modernization: Implications for US Navy Capabilities – Background and Issues for Congress in China-United States Economic and Geopolitical Relations, pp 187, Nova Science Publishers, 2007

34 A picture from the August 1997 issue of the PRC magazine Aerospace Knowledge shows a high-power microwave being used on troops.

35 Foreign Sources for PLA Laser Weapons Technology, http://www.globalsecurity.org/military/library/report/2004/04fisher/5hitech.htm

36 Russia developed Ranets E microwave beaming system way back in 2001 according to research work done of Guoqi Ni, Benqing Gao, Junwei Lu, Research on High Power Microwave weapons.

37 Richard D Fisher, China's Military Modernisation, Building for Regional and Global Reach, Greenwood Publishing, 2008

38 Richard Fisher, Jr., The PLA'S High-Tech Future Jamestown Foundation China Brief (Volume 1, Issue 4), http://www.strategycenter.net/research/pubID.9/pub_detail.asp

39 ibid

40 ibid

41 http://defence-update.com/20130518_lijian-sharp-sword-taxi.html

42 Ian M. Easton and L C Russell Hsiao, The Chinese People's Liberation Army's Unmanned Aerial Vehicle Project: Organizational Capacities and Operational Capabilities, pp 11 – 15, Project 2049 Institute, www.project2049.net

43 The ZOND-2 is a GLOBAL HAWK-size UAV that featured a large triangular phased array radar over the fuselage, while the ZOND-1 had the same aircraft with an under-fuselage synthetic aperture radar (SAR).

44 Richard D Fisher, China's Military Modernisation, Building for Regional and Global Reach, Greenwood Publishing, 2008

45 Global Security, Foreign Help For Hi-Tech Weapons http://www.globalsecurity.org/military/library/report/2004/04fisher/5hitech.htm

46 Ibid

47 http://minnickarticles.blogspot.in/2010/05/china-pushing-forward-on-uuvs.html

48 Richard D Fisher, China's Military Modernisation, Building for Regional and Global Reach, Greenwood Publishing, 2008

49 One 2007 report notes that China has "set up no fewer than 22 research institutes studying various aspects of electromagnetic launch (EML)."42 This report also notes that at the Thirteenth International Electromagnetic Launch Symposium, held in May2006 in Potsdam, Germany, the Chinese accounted for fifty-two papers, second only to the United States, which had seventy-two.

50 Richard D Fisher, China's Military Modernisation, Building for Regional and Global Reach, Greenwood Publishing, 2008

51. Richard Fisher, Jr., The PLA'S High-Tech Future Jamestown Foundation China Brief (Volume 1, Issue 4), http://www.strategycenter.net/research/pubID.9/pub_detail.asp

52. PLA's weapons that will blow your mind, http://www.defence.pk/forums/chinese-defence/128697-plas-weapons-will-blow-your-mind.html

53. http://en.wikipedia.org/wiki/Chinese_Information_Operations_and_Information_Warfare

54. C4ISR stands for command, control, communications, computers, intelligence, surveillance, and reconnaissance

55. Victor N Corpus, America's Acupuncture Points, http://www.atimes.com/atimes/China/HJ20Ad01.html

56. CNO is a broad term that has both military and civilian application and is deliberate actions taken to leverage and optimize these networks to gain information superiority and deny the enemy this enabling capability. CNO consists of computer network attack (CNA), computer network defence (CND) and computer network exploitation (CNE). CNA includes actions taken via computer networks to disrupt, deny, degrade, or destroy the information within computers and computer networks and/or the computers/networks themselves. CND includes actions taken via computer networks to protect, monitor, analyze, detect and respond to network attacks, intrusions, disruptions or other unauthorized actions that would compromise or cripple defence information systems and networks. CNE includes enabling actions and intelligence collection via computer networks that exploit data gathered from target or enemy information systems or networks. (http://en.wikipedia.org/wiki/Computer_network_operations)

57. IW as explained by Senior Colonel Wang Baocun and Li Fei of the Academy of Military Science, Beijing, in Liberation Army Daily, dated June 13 and June 20, 1995, http://en.wikipedia.org/wiki/Chinese_Information_Operations_and_Information_Warfare

58. Information dominance is defined as operational advantage gained from fully integrating the information functions, capabilities, and resources to optimize decision making and maximize war fighting effects.

59. Col Sanjeev Relia, Understanding Cyber Weapons, USI Journal, October-December 2013.

60. Mark A Stokes with Dean Cheng, China's Evolving Space Capabilities, Implication for US interests, Project 2049, April 2012

61. Ibid

62. Ian Easton, The Great Game in Space, China's Evolving ASAT Weapons Programs and Their Implications for Future US Strategy, Project 2049.

63. Bill Gertz, Strategic Military Satellites Vulnerable to Attack in Future Space War, Washington Free Beacon

64 Ian Easton, The Great Game In Space, Project 2049 paper,pp4

65 Rukhmani Gupta Ed, China Year Book 2012, IDSA publications 2013

66 http://en.wikipedia.org/wiki/Beidou_Navigation_Satellite_System

67 Richard D Fisher, China's Military Modernisation, Building for Regional and Global Reach, Greenwood Publishing, 2008

68 Global Security, Foreign Help For Hi-Tech Weapons http://www.globalsecurity.org/military/library/report/2004/04fisher/5hitech.htm

69 http://defensetech.org/2005/11/28/thermobaric-foes-explosive-threat/

70 A normal jet airplane engines has compressors (fans) to force in air which is mixed with fuel and ignited to generate a forward thrust. At supersonic speeds, an airplane's forward movement can generate ram pressure to force air into its engines. For vehicles traveling below Mach 4, the air inside a ramjet engine is slowed down to subsonic speeds. At higher speeds, the air flow can remain supersonic, resulting in an engine known as a scramjet.

71 Mark A Stokes with Dean Cheng, China's Evolving Space Capabilities, Project 2049 , April 2012

72 Ibid

73 Ibid

74 Richard D Fisher, China's Military Modernisation, Building for Regional and Global Reach, Greenwood Publishing, 2008

75 Global Security, Foreign Help For Hi-Tech Weapons http://www.globalsecurity.org/military/library/report/2004/04fisher/5hitech.htm

76 Richard D Fisher, China's Military Modernisation, Building for Regional and Global Reach, Greenwood Publishing, 2008

77 Richard D Fisher, China's Military Modernisation: Building for Regional and Global Reach, Praeger Security International, 2008

78 Ibid

79 Ibid

80 Ibid

81 Military and Security Developments Involving the People's Republic of China 2013, Annual Report to Congress,2013.

82 Ibid

83 PLA's weapons that will blow your mind, http://www.defence.pk/forums/chinese-defence/128697-plas-weapons-will-blow-your-mind.html

84. Military and Security Developments Involving the People's Republic of China 2013, Annual Report to Congress,2013.

85. Bill Gertz, Test is a past of New Arms Race for Superfast Weaponry, Jan 2013

86. China Conducts First Test of New Ultra-High Speed Missile Vehicle,http://missilethreat.com/china-conducts-first-test-of-new-ultra-high-speed-missile-vehicle/

87. Col Saif Ul Islam Khan, Hypersonic Weapons : Is India Prepared For the Next War? http://www.usiofindia.org/Article/?pub=Strategic%20Perspective&pubno=39&ano=2197

88. James Smith, China conducts First Test of Nano High Speed Space Missile Vehicle, Jan 2014

89. Richard Fisher, Jr., The PLA'S High-Tech Future Jamestown Foundation China Brief (Volume 1, Issue 4), http://www.strategycenter.net/research/pubID.9/pub_detail.asp

90. Richard D Fisher, China's Military Modernisation, Building for Regional and Global Reach, Greenwood Publishing, 2008

91. Rear Adm (Dr) S Kulshrestha .Chinese Advances in Nano-Technology,http://skulshrestha.com/military-strategy-fuels-chinas-leap-in-nanotechnology/

92. Ibid

93. Ibid

94. Richard D Fisher, China's Military Modernisation, Building for Regional and Global Reach, Greenwood Publishing, 2008

95. Rear Adm (Dr) S Kulshrestha .Chinese Advances in Nano-Technology,http://skulshrestha.com/military-strategy-fuels-chinas-leap-in-nanotechnology/

96. Biotechnology , http://en.wikipedia.org/wiki/Biotechnology

97. https://www.fas.org/irp/threat/prolif97/ne_asia.html

98. Richard D Fisher, China's Military Modernisation, Building for Regional and Global Reach, Greenwood Publishing, 2008

99. Ranjit Devraj, Biotechnology weapons was than nukes-Crain www.candreams.org/headlines02/0125-04.htm.

100. Micheal J Ainscough, Next Generation Bioweapons-Genetic Engineering and Biology Warfare, www.bibliotecgpleyades.net.cienca/cienca-virus08.htm

101. Ibid

102. PLA Develops Exoskeleton to Give Soldiers Superhuman Strength, http://goldsea.com/Text/index.php?id=14705

103. Want China Times, J-31 stealth fighter funded by PLA Air Force, not Navy: source, http://www.wantchinatimes.com/news-subclass-cnt.aspx?id=20131121000007&cid=1101

104 Global Security, Foreign Help For Hi-Tech Weapons http://www.globalsecurity.org/military/library/report/2004/04fisher/5hitech.htm

105 Richard D Fisher, China's Military Modernisation, Building for Regional and Global Reach, Greenwood Publishing, 2008

106 Ibid

107 http://rt.com/news/china-unveils-new-stealth-missile-frigate-485/

108 Plasma stealth is a process to use ionized gas (plasma) to reduce the radar cross section of an aircraft by interactions between EM radiation and ionized gas to form a layer or cloud of plasma to deflect or absorb radar, from simpler electrostatic or RF discharges to more complex laser discharges. http://en.wikipedia.org/wiki/Plasma_stealth

109 Richard D Fisher, China's Military Modernisation, Building for Regional and Global Reach, Greenwood Publishing, 2008

110 Ibid

111 http://en.wikipedia.org/wiki/VA-111_Shkval

112 Global Security, Foreign Help For Hi-Tech Weapons http://www.globalsecurity.org/military/library/report/2004/04fisher/5hitech.htm

113 Victor N Corpus, America's Acupuncture Points, http://www.atimes.com/atimes/China/HJ20Ad01.html

Countering The Dragon

"Observe calmly; secure our position; cope with affairs calmly; hide our capacities and bide our time; be good at maintaining a low profile; and never claim leadership."

—**Deng Xiaoping**

In April 2009, during the PLAN's sixtieth anniversary celebrations a senior Chinese Navy officer told USA representative. "As we develop our aircraft carriers why don't we reach an agreement, you and I. You take Hawaii East, we will take Hawaii West and the Indian Ocean. We will share information and we will save you all the trouble of developing your naval forces west of Hawaii".[1]

India is all too familiar with the 1962 "Hindi- Chini Bhai- Bhai" slogan and a back stab which left India bleeding. Deng Xiaoping's thoughts quoted above and the PLAN officer's remarks to USA bring no solace to the country which has suffered the Chinese military wrath. It is imperative that India studies, analyses and takes measures to counter the growing ambitions of China and the growing ability that transformation of its Armed forces brings to China. In examining trends in Chinese security and defence strategies, it's important to determine how they expect Indian military to respond.

China sees itself as a Great Power in Asia, and India as a major competitor. India has been working towards development of cordial relations with China and has focused on expanding economic ties and trade. The strategies the two nations appear to have for dealing with one another as assessed by an Australian Net Assessment Study on India and China brings out the following:-

China View on Dealing With India[2]

(a) A feigned indifference towards India coupled with denial that India is a potential rival.

(b) An effort to minimize direct conventional military competition with India, while subtly treating India as a significant nuclear threat.

(c) Maintenance of an enduring relationship with Pakistan while avoiding encouragement of Pakistan's revisionist policies towards India.

(d) Bolstering engagement with South/East Asian states while remaining engaged with smaller nations in South Asia.

(e) A continued focus on maintaining a high economic growth rate that generates a larger amount of resources for power-political purposes.

India View on Dealing With China[3]

(a) Avoid picking rhetorical, political or military fights with the Chinese and build confidence.

(b) Improve relations in areas where rapid improvement is possible, such as bilateral trade and fighting terrorism (extremism).

(c) Protect itself against the worst should relations sour. Nuclear deterrent, conventional force modernization, development of leading edge technologies such as IT, aviation, biotech and advanced materials manufacturing are used to ensure access to the best military capabilities.

(d) Revitalize relations with peripheral Asian states in Southeast and East Asia.

Other than being ancient civilizations, getting freed from foreign occupation at about the same period, China and India have many other striking similarities. Both States have seen periods of assertive international behaviour, including coercive diplomacy and conflicts with neighbouring countries. Historically, neither country has shown an expansionist tradition but have engaged with bordering tribes and states. Both countries embarked on economic reforms and are returning to a larger role in global politics.[4]

From the late forties, when India got its independence to the early sixties, the Indian Prime Minister Jawaharlal Nehru controlled the Indian Security policy making. Nehru, while seeking a role for India in world affairs, emphasized moral values and non-military engagements, and maintained non-aligned status for the country. Nehru downplayed external threats and sought global influence without military power. He was convinced that diplomacy could achieve the desired results. His politics resulted in the decline of Indian Armed Forces and the military was ill equipped with vintage weapons. The 1962 defeat was a shock and resulted insubstantial transformation in Indian strategic thinking. Military modernisation was now amongst National priorities. Military spending rose to an average of 3.6 percent of GDP in 1963-1973, and India showed a tilt towards USSR while still maintaining its non-aligned orientation.[5]

According to the Militarized International Disputes (MIDs) dataset, China was involved in the use of force (including war) more often than India between 1949 and 2001, eighty times for China, compared with forty nine times for India (Refer to Table 4).[6] The comparison clearly indicates fairly large use of force by the two countries, with China being nearly twice as aggressive as India. However, both have shown restraint as the economic development of the countries pushed them on the path of progress and development.

Border tensions between the two countries continue, flaring up once in a while. Despite media outbursts and rhetoric on both sides, the two governments down play the events and work to resolve it. In April 2013, border tensions between China and India flared after India claimed a contingent of 30 to 50 PLA soldiers crossed about 12 miles beyond the Line of Actual Control between the two countries and stayed there for three weeks. After a period of tensions, the two countries have decided on Border Defence and Cooperation Agreement to resolve border issues[7].

Military Modernisation

Both the countries have been developing their military forces incorporating high technology weapon modernisation programs, enhancement of power projection capabilities and doctrinal growth. The troops on the strength of the militaries in both countries are at Table5. The IISS 2013 assessment suggests that China's military manpower is nearly twice that of India. However, China in its projections has indicated that the PLA Army has fewer personnel than India. While both countries have same number of Commands, the numbers of Corps in PLA exceed Indian Army Corps by seven (Refer Table 6). China is considering reorganizing its seven military regions into five to be able to respond more swiftly to a crisis. This would be a shift from the current defence-oriented military to one that ensures more mobile and integrated management of the army, navy, air force and strategic missile units.[8] In addition to the integration of military regions, the PLA will also establish a joint operation command within each of the five military regions to coordinate all combat units from the Army, Air Force, Navy and Second Artillery Corps in a conflict.[9] This is a major step towards achieving integrated, informationalised operations in high tech battle environment.

As China re-structures and modernizes her force she seeks to also improve infrastructure that would support her operations. The infrastructural development of TAR has been substantial with China developing wide interlinking highways and suitably positioned airfields in the mountains. These have serious implications for India as the potential adversary can mobilize faster. The effect of PLA transformation, including dangers posed by the Assassin's Mace weapons, is discussed in succeeding paragraphs.

Maritime Power

The Indian Navy has long been a blue water force with reasonable power projection capabilities. PLAN has developed requisite assets, increased blue water experience since last decade. PLAN ships have been participating in international co-operative task's like anti-piracy.

PRC has modernized its surface fleet with the purchase of Sovremenny class destroyers, and production of sophisticated domestic designs of naval platforms. PLAN's destroyers are increasingly equipped with local hardware of more contemporary design and have better fire-control systems, stealth features, lower radar profile, lesser wake, improved C^{4}ISR systems and air defence equipment. Luyang-II destroyer possesses a sophisticated phased array radar system similar to western Aegis radars.[10] The Luyang Type 052C multirole destroyer has an indigenously developed four-array multifunction phased array radar and is also armed with the indigenous HQ-9 AD missile system.[11] PLAN is focusing on blue-water capabilities of conducting mobile operations and to enhancing its capabilities of strategic deterrence and counterattack. PLAN is in the forefront of China's A2/AD developments.

China's submarine fleet has also improved and the Song and Yuan-class submarines are quieter than their predecessors and the Kilo class submarines are equipped with two new-generation weapons, the Klub anti-ship cruise missile (ASCM) and Shkval torpedo. Some Chinese submarines, like Kilo and Yuan class submarines, with air-independent propulsion, can remain submerged for long durations. New diesel and nuclear-powered attack submarines have improved PLAN's undersea capabilities. A number of PLAN submarines are capable of firing ASCM. Underway replenishment capabilities have increased, enhancing the power projection capabilities manifold. China is expanding its access to logistics in the Indian Ocean and is likely to establish several access points in this area (potential sites include the Straits of Malacca, Lombok Strait, and Sunda Strait). These arrangements are likely to take the form of agreements for refueling, replenishment, crew rest and low-level maintenance.

The Marine Corps has developed an amphibious operational force comprising of LHA, LPDs, LCACs and helicopters for stand-off operations. Amphibious armoured vehicles will enhance Marine Corps operational capabilities. China has nearly twice the number of principal surface combat platforms compared to India. PLAN has a reasonable amphibious capability with options to undertake ship to shore operations using sea and air route. (Refer Table 7).In 2014, China's amphibious ship, along-with two guided missile destroyers, conducted exercises in IOR.[12] It has been reported that India is looking to improve its amphibious capabilities by increasing the number of LPDs to four. LPD class of ships will enhance India's strategic reach.[13]

The Chinese naval buildup is a matter of concern for Indian security. To maintain its dominance in the IOR, Indian Navy has two aircraft carriers and is, in addition, constructing next-generation warships. The Indian Navy has also launched several new projects to beef up its fleet of stealth frigates. The lead vessels are the Shivalik class of frigates.

India has obtained nuclear powered submarines (INS Chakra) on lease from Russia. The indigenous Arihant nuclear-powered submarine has given a boost to the Navy, making the Indian Navy more vibrant and stronger. With the Chinese Navy advancing and extending reach in IOR, India must develop capabilities to address South China Sea. India has to focus on increasing the operational range of its fleets. Accordingly, India has been investing in underway replenishment ships and has acquired capable tankers to replenish its blue water navy while out at sea.

The Indian naval platforms have shown rapid improvement in striking power, air defence and stealth of surface ships. Further improvements are necessary to cater for strikes by UCPs and anti-ship missiles. India will need to improve the anti-submarine warfare capabilities in view of China's submarine modernisation and develop counter measures against under water attacks by bottom rising mines, super-cavitation under water weapons while incorporating electronic defence measures to neutralize robot fish swarms.

Aerospace

PLAAF is following a structured transformation plan to meet the strategic requirements of conducting both offensive and defensive air operations. PLAAF focus is on reconnaissance and early warning, air strike, air and missile defence, and strategic projection. New-generation fighters and new-type of ground-to-air missiles and radar systems, improvement in its early warning, command and communications networks, and raising its strategic early warning, strategic deterrence and long-distance air strike capabilities are PLAAF thrust areas[14]. A thrust in Air defence has resulted in a shift from point defence of vulnerable points to a new Joint Anti-Air Raid Campaign doctrine[15] based on a modern, integrated air defence system capable of effective offensive counter-air and defensive counter-air. PLAAF offensive capabilities have increased with its acquisition of increasing number of 3rd, 4th and 5th generation aircraft outfitted with long-range, precision strike weapons for land attack and anti-ship missions with in-flight refueling capabilities (Refer Table 8). Two fifth-generation aircraft J-20 and J-31 are currently under development. It has been stated that one of these, i.e. J-20, is likely to enter service by 2018.[16] Acquisition, production, purchase of AWACS, AEW&C aircraft (KJ-2000[17] and KJ-200) and the refueling aircraft, H-6U[18], significantly extend the ranges of the modern air fleet. China has its own version of Su-30 (the J-16) but with enhanced stealth features will further enhance her strike capability.[19] With these modern weapons PLAAF could attempt to strike targets deep into Indian territory.

The UAV systems are likely to emerge as the critical enabler for PLA long range precision strike missions within a 3000 kilometer radius of Chinese shores.[20] China has taken long strides in UAVs and UCAVs development and has also converted their fleet of retired J-6s into unmanned attack fighters.[21]

Chinese AF has acquired capabilities of deep strike as has been discussed. PLAAF reach can be negated by deploying capable fighters and effective Air Defence. The IAF had inducted its first Su-30 squadron at Tezpur in northern Assam in June 2009. Two Sukhoi 30MKI squadrons have been placed each at Tezpur and Chabua in Assam[22] and guarding these assets are eight Akash air defence squadrons which shall be deployed in Arunachal Pradesh by 2015.

India needs to improve the teeth of its Air Force. It has been reported that India has shown interest in developing Fifth Generation Fighter Aircraft with Russia.[23] India is developing a next-generation fighter of its own–the Advanced Medium Combat Aircraft (AMCA). Defence Research and Development Organization (DRDO) displayed a large-scale model of the AMCA at Aero India 2013 in February, in Bengaluru.[24] Indian Air Force has extended its operational reach by acquiring midair refueling capabilities for its fighter aircraft. Development of additional suitably positioned airfields and advance landing grounds will increase strike options. The acquisition of transport aircraft from US has increased India's Strategic lift capabilities.

There is a requirement to improve early warning capabilities and ability to pick up stealth aircrafts and UAV strikes. India should consider operationalising OTH and 3D Radars integrated with survivable AD control System with strike and counter strike capabilities.

China used a medium-range ballistic missile to shoot down one of its own aging satellites, a Chinese Feng Yun 1C polar orbit weather satellite that it had launched into orbit in 1999. Formation of an Integrated Space Cell was announced by Defence Minister AK Antony who is reported to have said that it was being established due to "the growing threat" to India's space assets. He said that "Offensive counter-space systems like anti-satellite weaponry, new classes of heavy-lift and small boosters and an improved array of military space systems have emerged in our neighborhood," and stressed on the necessity of countering these developments. The announcement by the Defence Minister clearly addressed India's concern of PLA Space war capabilities and the need to counter them. Though Indian counter space program may be at a relatively nascent phase, it shows India's resolve to not be deterred by PLA transformation but evolve a counter to each development by the PLA. India is in the process of setting up a Space Command for its Armed Forces.[25] India's military capability remains the key for ensuring security and stability in relations with China.[26]

Realigning Land Forces for Modern Warfare

The PLA ground forces reorientation from theater defence to trans-theater mobility is due to the strategic need for mobility and multi-dimensional operations. PLA ground forces modernisation plans center on the development of army aviation troops, light mechanized units and special operations force, and building up of digitalized units. Unit trends are towards a small, modular and multi-functional set up with enhanced capabilities for air-ground integrated operations, long-distance maneuvers, rapid assaults and special operations.[27] The PLA mobile operational units include 18 Combined Corps, plus additional independent combined operational divisions and brigades.[28] The PLA ground forces field a full range of equipment, including tanks, armored personnel carriers, artillery, SSMs, SAMs, helicopters and UAVs in large numbers, Electronic warfare and surveillance equipment, wheeled and amphibious AFVs and Missile Forces are also technolgically advanced. The trend towards special-mission battalions has led to the formation of 'combined battalions', i.e., battalion battle groups formed from company-sized units from up to a dozen different branches of the armed forces.[29] The mechanized brigade are seen as the principal operational formation for the future.

PLA is expanding its force of ballistic missiles (long-range and short-range), cruise missiles and is giving impetus to firepower and amphibious operations.[30] PLA ground forces have been focussing on improving the ability of the forces to project power to the peripheries, by using a combination of military and civilian transport infrastructure. The synergistic use of civil-military transport assisted by the developments in infrastructure allows the PLA to deploy its key formations faster, enhancing its ability to consolidate control in remote regions and also to develop offensive operations. In the conventional field, the Second Artillery, which had no conventional missiles till 1985, now has the largest conventional missile arsenal in the Asia-Pacific.[31] They also have 200-500 Ground Launched Cruise Missiles.

Missile force serves as a force multiplier and increases the lethality of attacks. The numbers of missile continue to grow indicating the importance China is giving to its missile warfare. SRBM numbers have increased from being just 30 per cent in 2000 to 50 per cent of Second Artillery missile system. Much to India's concern, China has one of the largest arsenals of cruise missiles. The missiles per launcher have also increased for both the SRBMs and the GLCMs. The ICBM count has increased from 5 per cent to nearly 14 per cent and may grow further as China develops new variants like the DF 31/31-A and DF-41, constantly increasing the range and maneuverability. The number of IRBM held on PLA inventory may have decreased but the 21C and 21D MRBMs have increased substantially. India's concerns are bound to increase as large numbers of MRBMs are deployed in Tibet.

ICBMs are being modernized to the newer version of DF-31 and DF-31A. The DF-31 is available in three variants: road mobile DF-31, road mobile DF-31A with extended range, and the submarine launched JL-2 SLBM. China is developing reasonable ballistic missile defence umbrella consisting of kinetic energy intercept at exo-atmospheric altitudes (>80km), as well as intercepts of ballistic missiles and other aerospace vehicles within the upper atmosphere. In January 2010, and again in January 2013, China successfully intercepted a ballistic missile at mid-course, using a ground-based missile.[32] China is likely to use these Shashoujian in future campaigns for maximum effects or gains.

The Indian Armed Forces are undergoing a process of transformation with acquisition of sophisticated weapon systems to survive and dominate the net-centric battlefield of the future.³³ India has been concerned over the changes in Chinese MR, infrastructural development, military modernization etc. In a journal it was brought out that Gen VK Singh, Chief of Army Staff, stated publicly for the first time, that the Army would 'reorganize, restructure and relocate' various formations to help transform it into a more agile and lethal force.³⁴ It was brought out that India has completed raising of two new Mountain Divisions for the Eastern Command, which are to be deployed against China. It has been reported that Indian 4 Corps is responsible for the Kameng sector in western Arunachal Pradesh, with three Mountain Divisions, and Rangapahar-based 3 Corps will be in charge of eastern Arunachal Pradesh with three Mountain Divisions. A new Mountain Strike Corps, comprising two additional mountain divisions, could be created by 2015-20. A fourth Artillery Division could be introduced to support the new Mountain Strike Corps. Reports suggest that two additional Independent Mountain Brigades are to be raised - one each for Ladakh and Uttarakhand. The planned new raisings would add about 100,000 troops to the existing Indian Army deployments aimed at the Chinese in the northeast of the country.³⁵

The Indian Government has sanctioned the raising of one Mountain Strike Corps.³⁶ The troops are expected to be equipped with significant capabilities like high technology weapons, strategic move capabilities, meaningful air defence cover and fire support as also necessary gear to operate at high altitudes.

It can be appreciated that an increase in combat potential in a theatre of operations will require a proportionate increase by the adversary to create a balance. When considered in mountainous terrain, the factor of proportionality is very high. Thus, it will be relatively easier for India, as a Nation with no aggressive intent, to raise defensive forces and restructure/redeploy formations and take its defence preparedness to a level that would negate PLA's aggressive designs and transformations. Force-on-force proportionality aids in defence against conventionally armed forces. However, against high technology warfare there would be a requirement to develop meaningful asymmetries.

China's high technology development, development of large number of missiles, including SRBM, progress on IW, EW, space and stealth are of serious concern for India. While India has been able to maintain a reasonable parity to counter conventional attacks and deter nuclear war, the

Assassin's Mace and asymmetric warfare capabilities remain a concern. The induction of Assassin's Mace weaponry introduces an asymmetry, a new contingency which India would need to factor in its operational planning. India has to address the asymmetry caused by Shashoujian by incorporating requisite capabilities not only in the Mountain Strike Corps but in its military forces as a whole.

The Mountain Strike Corps being raised needs to be suitably equipped. Not only should the soldiers be equipped with high tech weaponry they must also have laser detection and counter lasing capabilities as well as low thermal signature clothing and weapons. The fighting formations need to be provided information and control from UAVs and space assets, and be capable of working in an electromagnetically intense environment infested with information attacks. The fire support for operations must be from a mix of weapons capable of launching fire assaults over long distances. There is a requirement to have strategic mobility, ability for airborne and heli-borne operations inbuilt in the Mountain Strike Corps. There is also a need to have over the horizon detection capabilities in addition to conventional early warning radars operating different bands of frequencies with inbuilt counter measures. Ballistic Missile Defence and Ground Based Air Defence need a boost. OTH and 3D radar with quick reaction, medium to long range surface to air missiles and fire control guns need to be positioned. India could consider raising Army Air Defence Divisions for the Northern, Central and Eastern Sectors facing China. The defence research organisations and other establishments in India are reported to be working on high tech military equipment, deployment of which needs to be hastened.

To counter the Ballistic Missile threat from China India needs to have a credible Ballistic Missile Program. The then DRDO Chief VK Saraswat told the press on March 21, 2010, that the Ballistic Missile System in India is being developed in two phases under a capability based deployment plan. In the first phase, DRDO will develop and deploy a system for defence against missiles with less than 2,000 km range like Pakistan's Ghauri and Shaheen missiles. In the second phase, system capability will be upgraded to defend against missiles with ranges greater than 2,000 km that can additionally deploy decoys or maneuver. The Phase 2 missile defence system will be based on the AD-1 and AD-2 interceptor missile that are currently under development. These interceptors would be capable of shooting down missiles that have ranges greater than 5,000 km, which follow a distinctly different trajectory than a missile with a range of 2,000 km or less. The Phase 2 system will match the capability of the THAAD or Terminal High Altitude Area Defence missiles deployed by the United States as part of its missile shield.[37] The missile shield once in place will safeguard India from the plethora of missile that PLA is acquiring in its modernisation drive. Ballistic Missile Defence systems need to be EMP hardened, with adequate electronic counter measures in-built. It should be integrated with nationwide control and reporting systems put in place by the Indian Air Force.

A counter strike capability is as important as development of Ballistic Missile Defence. For surface to surface engagement the Indian Armed Forces have inducted Agni I (700 km), Agni II (2000 km) and Agni III (3500 km) capable of reaching most of China.[38] It has been reported that India is also planning to extend its missile coverage of China by deploying 3500 km Agni-III and the under development 5000 km Agni-V as soon as possible. This would address the heart land of China and interfere with mobilization, deployment and redeployment of PLA.

Both the countries are nuclear weapon states, with China possessing larger number of these arsenals. India needs to have a triad of nuclear weapons, with its resources well dispersed, in nuclear hardened emplacements or at sea with control arrangements capable of operating in intense EM environment for credible nuclear deterrence and second strike capability.

The India Naval platforms should have stealth features for low signatures and latest antisubmarine warfare and air defence capabilities as also the ability to operate silently under water over long distances, as discussed earlier. There is a requirement to give a boost to amphibious capabilities. Procurement of LHA by India and raising of Indian Marines by Army, to operate under the Army or directly under Integrated Defence Staff along with greater number of strategic lift aircraft are necessary for enhancing power projection abilities. India should look at the possibility of developing bases in friendly countries in Western Pacific to permanently position naval assets. Creation of Chief of Defence Staff is considered essential for meaningful development of integrated operations structure in the country.

As mentioned earlier, India should not try a force-on-force development of its military but look at building asymmetries. Indian force development should provide enhanced deterrence and greater survivability. India has embarked on the road of restructuring its forces and equipping them for future wars. The armed forces are in the process of creation of three new Tri-Service Commands to handle Space, Cyber and Special Forces. These three components are critical in deploying capabilities for conventional and asymmetric warfare.[39] In addition to modernisation of its military, DEWs remain one of the focus areas along with space security, cyber security and hypersonic vehicle.[40] Indo-Russian venture underway to develop a hypersonic missile Brahmos 2 [41] capable of flying between 5 to 7 Mach[42] would provide India not only counter strike ability but would also act as deterrence.[43]

As part of the technology roadmap, DRDO scientists are working on developing a satellite to monitor electronic communications across the border. Communication-Centric Intelligence Satellite being developed by Defence Electronics Research Laboratory is likely to be launched in 2015.[44] India has launched its military satellite, GSAT-7 Rukmini, which will facilitate networking amongst warships, submarines and aircraft allowing maritime threats to be detected and countered in quick time.[45] GSAT-7A likely to be launched by IAF will link AWACS, aircraft and ground and air based radars. It has been reported that India is planning networks of small, less expensive satellites and systems.[46] DRDO is working towards enhancing self-reliance in defence systems and production of world class weapon systems and equipment for the Indian Armed Forces.

An engagement at diplomatic and military levels aids in maintenance of peace in the region and is a recommended action. The value of military participation in engagement activities cannot be overstated. Application of the engagement process with clearly identified aims and objectives; and accurate situational awareness enables deterrence of potential flash points and regional stability. A policy of focused engagement, maintenance of equilibrium in South/East Asia, centered on the alliances with important regional players like Japan, Korea, Vietnam, Indonesia, Australia, and others will continue to put pressure on China's autocratic political system and she will hesitate to expand her empire. Though the two Nations, India and China, have aired their desire to resolve areas of divergence but incoherence in actions, derails the process. India must have a carefully formulated long-term policy of engagement with China and the policy should be progressed vigorously whilst China needs to match words with action, to enable peace and stability in the region.

Endnotes

1. Country Review "Strategic Digest Vol 39" November 2009 pp1322

2. Brig Mick Ryan, India-China in 2030, A Net Assessment of Competition of two Rising Powers, October 2012.

3. Ibid

4. George J. Gilboy, Eric Heginbotham, Chinese And Indian Strategic Behaviour, Growing Power And Alarm, Cambridge University Press. pp xv

5. Ibid, pp 43

6. Ibid, pp 75

7. Jeff M. Smith, On Sino-Indian Border, Status-Quo Unacceptable, http://thediplomat.com/2013/11/on-sino-indian-border-status-quo-unacceptable

8. The Japan Times, China considers revamping military regions: report, http://www.japantimes.co.jp/news/2014/01/01/asia-pacific/china-considers-revamping-military-regions-report/#.UuPYbdK6Zdg

9. Want China Times, Four of China's military regions will be merged into two: source, http://www.wantchinatimes.com/news-subclass-cnt.aspx?id=20140102000077&cid=1101

10. The People's Liberation Army Navy: A Modern Navy with Chinese characteristics, Aug 2009, http://www.fas.org/agency/oni/pla_navy.pdf.

11. http://www.sinodefence.com/navy/surface/type052c_luyang2.asp

12. People's Daily online, http://eng.chinamil.com.cn/news-channels/pla-daily-commentary/2014-01/24/content_5748767.htm

13. Indian Navy to induct four more Landing Platform Docks, http://www.domain-b.com/defence/sea/indian_navy/20110214_platform.html

14. Defence White Paper, "The Diversified Employment of China's Armed Forces" Xinhua, 2013.

15. David Axe "Stealth Fighter or Bomber" The Diplomat, 26 July 2011 <www.andrewerick son.com/2011/07/David-axe-on-j-20-in diplomat>

16 Jim Wolf, New Chinese fighter jet expected by 2018: U.S. intelligence, Reuters, May 21, 2010. Also, see Military Balance 2012, p. 212.

17 KJ-2000 is a Airborne Early Warning and Control system comprising domestically designed electronics and radars installed on a modified Ilyushin IL-76 airframe

18 China is reported looking for its replacements. IL78, Y-20, modified for the role are possible choices.

19 James Dunnigan, China Celebrates Another Grand Theft, http://www.strategypage.com/dls/articles/China-Celebrates-Another-Grand-Theft-1-14-2013.asp accessed on January 15, 2013

20 Ian M. Easton and L.C. Russell Hsiao, The Chinese People's Liberation Army's Unmanned Aerial Vehicle Project: Organizational Capacities and Operational Capabilities, Project 2049 Institute, March 11, 2013, p 3

21 Global Security Org dated January 7, 2013. http://www.globalsecurity.org/wmd/library/news/china/2013/china-130107-cna01.htm?_m=3n%2e002a%2e700%2eer0a o00dsz%2emxo accessed on January 8, 2013

22 PTI, Army planning to set up mountain strike corps, Aug 2011, <www.zeenews.India.com/news/nation/army planning to set up mountain strike corps.html>

23 Sukhoi/HAL FGFA, http://en.wikipedia.org/wiki/Sukhoi/HAL_FGFA

24 Vladimir Karnozov, Indian 'Home-Grown' AMCA, An Alternative To FGFA, http://www.ainonline.com/aviation-news/paris-air-show/2013-06-13/indian-home-grown-amca-alternative-fgfa

25 Rahul Bedi, India Confirms Joint Commands For Cyber, Special Forces And Space, http://www.janes.com/article/28473/india-confirms-joint-commands-for-cyber-special-forces-and-space

26 Capt Antony George NM "Deployment of PLA Navy Ships in Gulf of Aden for Contrary privacy: Ramifications for India "CNW Journal Annual Issue 2009"

27 China's National Defence, White Paper, Beijing PRC; Information Office of the State Council of the People's Republic of China, 2010.

28 China's National Defence, White Paper on the Diversified Employment of China's Armed Forces 2013, Beijing PRC; Information Office of the State Council of the People's Republic of China, 2013

29 China's National Defence, White Paper on the Diversified Employment of China's Armed Forces 2013, Beijing PRC; Information Office of the State Council of the People's Republic of China, 2013

30 Infantry fighting vehicles<www.ausairpower.net/APA-PLA-AFV.html>

31 IISS, Military Balance 2012, Chapter 6

32 Ibid

33. Kaza Latindra "Dragon in Space : Implication for India" Air power journal vol 3 No.3 Monsoon 2008 pp95.

34. Nitin Gokhale, India's Doctrinal shift ?,The Diplomat Jan 2011www.the-diplomat.com/2011/02/09/India's Doctrinal Shift India's Offensive Strategy 02/09.

35. Khan Sufyan<www.the-diplomat.com/2011/01/25/Indias Doctrinal Shift Indias Offensive Strategy 01/25>.

36. Kapil Patil, India's New Mountain Strike Corps: Conventional Deterrence, http://thediplomat.com/2013/08/indias-new-mountain-strike-corps-conventional-deterrence/

37. Country Review "Strategic Digest, Volume 39" November 2009 pp 1314.

38. Rajat Pandit "With China in mind, Agni V Test scheduled for Dec" The Times of India, June 04, 2011, pp 13.

39. Rajat Pandit, Tri-service commands for space, cyber warfare, http://timesofindia.indiatimes.com/india/Tri-service-commands-for-space-cyber-warfare/articleshow/20115462.cms

40. DRDO's Director General Dr. V.K. Saraswat as quoted in India's DRDO: Developing Weapons of the Future, http://www.2point6billion.com/news/2010/08/03/india%E2%80%99s-drdo-developing-weapons-of-the-future-6610.html

41. "Dr A Sivathanu Pillai, CEO and MD for BAIL, has stated said that Brahmos 2 Hypersonic vehicles with multi-use will reduce the cost of putting payload in the orbit. It could deliver the payload at multiple points and it can come back" as quoted by Virendra Singh Ghunawat, India to have Sudarshan Chakra-like missile soon, *India Today* http://indiatoday.intoday.in/story/sudarshan-chakra-brahmos-aerospace-india-ltd-bail-air-to-air-missile/1/325940.html

42. BrahMos-II, http://en.wikipedia.org/wiki/BrahMos-II

43. Col Saif Ul Islam Khan, Hypersonic Weapons : Is India Prepared For the Next War? http://www.usiofindia.org/Article/?pub=Strategic%20Perspective&pubno=39&ano=2197

44. Vivek Raghuvanshi, India's Tech Roadmap Points to Small Sats, Space Weapons, http://www.defensenews.com/article/20130910/DEFREG03/309100007/India-s-Tech-Roadmap-Points-Small-Sats-Space-Weapons

45. Ibid

46. Ibid

Table1

US Forces In Japan

Table contains figurative data of US forces in Japan as given in IISS 2013 report and supports the analysis given in Chapter I.

Japan	Location	Strength
US Army: 1 HQ (9th Theatre Army Area Comd)	Zama	2,500
US Navy		6,750
• 1 HQ (7th Fleet) & 1 base	Yokosuka	
• 1 base	Sasebo	
Equipment by Type - 1 CVN: 2 CGHM: 3 DDGHM: 4 DDGM: 1 LCC: 4 MCO: 1 LHD: 1 LDP: 1 LSD		
USMC	Okinawa	14,950
Forces by Role		
• 1 Marine Div (3rd)		
• 1 Ftr Sqn with 12 F/A-18D Hornet		
• 1 Tkr Sqn with 12 KC-130J Hercules		
• 2 Tpt Hel Sqn with 12 CH-46E Sea Knight		
• 1 Tpt Hel Sqn with 12 MV-22B Osprey		
• 3 Tpt Hel Sqn with CH-53E Sea Stallion		
Total		**36,700**

US Air Force		12,500
Forces by Role		
• 1 HQ (5th Air Force)	Okinawa – Kadena AB	
• 2 Ftr Sqn with 18 F-16C/D Fighting Falcons	Misawa AB	

• 1 Ftr Wg with
  • 1 AEW&C Sqn with 2 E-3B Sentry
  • 1 CSAR Sqn with 8 HH-60G Pave Hawk
  • 2 Ftr Sqn with 24 F-15C/D Eagle
	Kadena AB	

• 1 Tpt Wg with 10 C-130H Hercules & 3 Beech 1900C (C-12J)	Yokota AB	
• Special Ops Gp	Okinawa - Kadena AB	

Table 2

US Forces In Republic of Korea

Table contains figurative data of US forces in Republic of Korea as given in IISS 2013 report and supports the analysis given in Chapter I.

Republic of Korea	Location	Strength
US Army		19,200
Forces by Role		
• 1 HQ (8th Army)	Seoul	
• 1 Div HQ (2nd Inf) • 1 Armd HBCT • 1 CBT Avn Bde • 1 Arty Bde • 1 AD Bde	Tongduchon	
Equipment by Type: M1 Abrams; M2/M3 Bradley; M 109; M270 MRLS; AH-64 Apache; CH-47 Chinook; UH-60 Black Hawk; MIM-104 Patriot/ FIM-92A Avenger; 1 (APS) HBCT Set		
US Navy		250
USMC		250
Total		28,500
US Air Force	Location	Strength
Forces by Role		
• 1 HQ (7th Air Force)	Osan AB	

• 1 Ftr Wg
   • 1 Ftr Sqn with 20 F-16C/D Fighting Falcon
   • 1 Ftr Sqn with 24 A-10C Thunderbolt II
   • 1 ISR Sqn with U-2S
	Osan AB	

• 1 Ftr Wg
   • 1 Ftr Sqn with 20 F-16 C/D Fighting Falcon
   • 1 Spl Ops Sqn
	Kusan AB	

Table 3

US Forces In Pacific Ocean and Australia

Table contains figurative data of US forces in Pacific Ocean and Australia as given in IISS 2013 reports and support the analysis given in Chapter I.

Pacific Ocean and Australia	Location	Strength
US Pacific Command – US Navy, 3rd Fleet		
Equipment by Type - 8 SSBN; 19 SSGN; 8 SSN; 5 CVN; 11 CGHM; 18 DDGHM; 6 DDGM; 9 FFH; 3 FFHM; 2 MCO; 3 LHD; 1 LHA; 3 LPD; 4 LSD		
US Southern Command – US Navy 4th Fleet		
Equipment by Type – 1 FFH		
Guam		4,300
US Pacific Command • 1 Air Base • 1 Naval Base		
Equipment by Type – 2 SSGN; 1 SSN; 1 MPS Sqn (MPS-3 with equipment for one MEB) with 4 Logistics & Support Vessels		
Australia		180
• 1 SEWS • 1 Communication Facility • 1 SIGINT Stn	Pine Gap	

Table 4

China And India (1949-2001): Use Of Force And War

	Number of Cases		Cases Per Year	
	China	India	China	India
Use of Force				
1949 – 1979	57	26	1.84	0.84
1980 – 2001	19	19	0.86	0.86
Total 1949 – 2001	76	45	1.43	0.85
War				
1949 – 1979	3	3	0.10	0.10
1980 – 2001	1	1	0.05	0.05
Total 1949 – 2001	4	4	0.08	0.08
Total Force and War				
1949 – 1979	60	29	1.94	0.94
1980 – 2001	20	20	0.91	0.91
Total 1949 – 2001	80	49	1.51	0.92

Source : Correlates of War (CoW) Militarized International Disputes (MIDs) 3.1 dataset, 1816-2001, accessible at http://www.correlatesofwar.rog/. Data in the table includes "use of force" (code "4") and "war" (code "5") in the MIDs data set.

Table 5

Sino-India Armed Forces Comparison

Table contains figurative data of China PLA manpower and supports the analysis given in Chapter V.

	China	**India**
Active Troops		
Army	1,600,000 *(850,000)* *	1,129,900
Air force	300,000 – 330,000 *(398,000)* *	127,200
Navy	255,000 *(235,000)* *	58,350
Strategic Missile Forces	100,000	-
Paramilitary	660,000	1,322,150
Coast Guard	-	9,550
Total Source: The Military Balance 2013, IISS	**2,285,000**	**1,322,150**

*As per the Chinese White Paper on Defence 2013

Table 6

Sino-India Armed Forces Structure Comparison

Table contains figurative data of China PLA and supports the analysis given in Chapter V.

	China	India
Commands		
MACs/ Command	7	7 incl ARTRAC
Combined Corps HQ	18	
Strike Corps HQ		3
Holding Corps HQ		10
Special Forces	7 Units	8 Units
Source: The Military Balance 2013, IISS		

Table 7

Sino-India Navy Comparison

Table contains figurative data of China PLA and supports the analysis given in Chapter V.

	China	India
Submarines		
Strategic: SSBN	4	
Tactical		
SSN	5	1
SSK	55	14
SSB/ SSI	1	
Principal Surface Combatants		
Aircraft Carrier	1	1(2)*
Destroyer: DDGHM	12	6
Destroyer: DDGM	2	5
Frigate: FFGHM	29	11
Frigate: FFGH	1	
Frigate: FFGM/ HM	4	
Frigate: FFG	28	
Frigate: FFH		1
Amphibious Platform		
LPD	2	1
LSM	59	5
LST	26	5

Source: The Military Balance 2013, IISS, * second carrier has joined Indain Navy

Table 8

Sino-India Air Force Comparison

This Table contains figurative data of China PLA and supports the analysis given in Chapter V.

	China	India
Aircraft		
BBR	82	
FTR	842	63
FGA	543	736
ATK	120	
EW	13	
ELINT	4	
AEW&C	8	3
C2	5	
TKR (AAR)	10	6
TPT	326	238
TRG	950	241
ISR		3
Source: The Military Balance 2013, IISS		

* <u>Note</u>.　PLA has approx 600 helicopters as of 2012 MI 17(212), S-70 'Black Hawk'(19), Z-8(33), Z-9(269), Z-10(24), Z-19(12)[1] while India has about 350 (Source: The Military Balance 2013, IISS)

Endnotes

1　www.chinadefence-mashup.com/the pla army helicopter number close to 600.html "The PLA Army helicopter number close to 600"

Index

A

Active Defence vii, 34

Advanced Multirole Combat Aircraft xv

Air Based Shashoujian xv, 23, 41, 47, 48, 55, 59, 62

Air Based Shashoujian (ABS) 23, 41

Airborne Warning and Control System xv

Aircraft Carrier 28, 96

Air Defence Identification Zone xv, 7, 8, 28, 38

Aksai Chin 11

Anti Access 12

Anti-Satellite xv, 27, 32, 37, 41, 42, 43, 44, 48, 54, 55, 65, 68, 79

Anti Satellite Missile 22

Anti-Ship ballistic missile xv, 32, 46

Anti-Ship Cruise missile xv

Area Denial 12, 32

Art of War 3, 24

ASEAN xv, 9

ASEAN Regional Forum 9

Asia-Pacific 10, 12, 13, 14, 35, 80

Assassin's Mace i, iii, v, vii, viii, ix, x, xi, xiii, 3, 5, 6, 8, 9, 18, 20, 21, 22, 23, 24, 25, 26, 27, 28, 31, 33, 37, 40, 42, 47, 52, 64, 75, 82. *See also* **Shashoujian**

Trends v

Assassin's Mace Weapons ix, 5

Association of Southeast Asian Nations xv

asymmetric warfare vii, 3, 14, 19, 82, 84

B

Ballistic Missile Defence 46, 82, 83

Beijing University of Aeronautics and Astronautics 50, 58

C

Cam Ranh Bay Port 12

Carrier Battle Groups xv, 13, 27, 30

Centers of Gravity xv, 21

Central Asian Republics xv, 11

Centre for Strategic and International Studies xvi, 2, 15

China Aerospace Science and Industry Corporation xv, 54

Chinese Communist Party xv, 4, 5, 6, 7, 10, 53

Chinese Military Modernisation ix, xiii

Chittagong 11

Command, control, communications, computers, intelligence, surveillance and reconnaissance (C4ISR) xv, 46, 52, 68, 76

Commissions of Science, Technology and Industry for National Defence 41

Computer Network Attacks 29

Computer Network Operations xv

Cyber warfare 31

Cyber weapons 53

D

Deng Xiaoping 4, 14, 25, 72

Diego Garcia 12

Directed Energy Weapon xvi, 31, 41

E

Economic Cooperation Framework Agreement of 2010 8

Electro Magnetic Pulse vi, xvi, 40, 44, 45, 46, 47, 54, 66, 83

Electronic Warfare xvi, 29, 52

F

Falkland wars x

Fuel Air Explosives xvi, 55

G

Ghauri and Shaheen missiles 82

Gilgit-Baltistan region 11

Great Wall 19

Gwadar 11

H

Hambantota 11

Harbin Institute of Technology 58

High Power Microwave xvi, 46, 47, 48, 66, 67

Hu Jintao 1, 8

Human Wave attacks 19

I

Indian Ocean Region xvi, 3, 10, 11, 33, 47, 76, 77

Information Warfare xvi, 22, 29, 30, 31, 33, 51, 52, 60

    Computer Network Attacks 29

    Deception 29

    Electronic Warfare xvi, 29, 52

    Precision Strike Warfare 29

    Psychological Warfare 19, 29

Intercontinental Ballistic Missile xvi, 56, 80

Intermediate Range Ballistic Missile xvi, 35, 36

Iran-Iraq war x

K

Key point strikes vii

KMT regime 9

Korean peninsula 8

Kosovo Campaign x

Kuomintang xvi

L

Land Attack Cruise Missiles xvi

Land-Attack Cruise Missiles 35

Land Based Shashoujian (LBS) xvi, 23, 41, 42, 43, 45, 47, 48, 51, 55, 59, 62

Landing Craft Air Cushion xvi

Landing Platform Dock xvi

Laser weapons 41

Line of Actual Control xvi, 11, 74

Lombok Strait 76

M

Maneuverable re-entry vehicles xvii, 32, 33

Mao Zedong 1, 15, 18, 24, 40

Medium Range Ballistic Missile xvii, 35, 36

Militarized International Disputes 74, 93

Ming Dynasty 19

Multiple Independently Targetable Re-entry Vehicle xvii

N

Nanjing University of Aeronautics and Astronautics 58

Nanjing University of Science and Technology 58

Nano-Technology 59, 70

National Reconnaissance Office 44

National University of Defence Technology 58

Nuclear Deterrence 34

Nuclear EMP attacks 44

O

Oceanic Strike xvii

Oceanic Strike Shashoujian (OSS) xvii, 23, 41, 45, 48, 49, 59, 62

Okinawa 12, 88, 89

Over The Horizon xvii, 35, 78, 82

P

Pacific Ocean vi, 12, 92

People's Liberation Army vii, viii, ix, x, xi, xvii, 1, 5, 14, 18, 19, 22, 23, 25, 26, 27, 30, 33, 34, 35, 40, 41, 42, 43, 44, 46, 48, 49, 50, 51, 52, 53, 54, 55, 56, 57, 58, 59, 61, 62, 64, 65, 67, 68, 69, 70, 74, 75, 78, 79, 80, 81, 83, 85, 86, 94, 95, 96, 97

People's Liberation Army (Air Force) x, xvii, 22, 35, 48, 77, 78

People's Liberation Army (Navy) x

People's Republic of China xvii, 1, 2, 7, 15, 16, 20, 34, 38, 39, 50, 51, 62, 64, 65, 67, 69, 70, 75, 86

PLAAF Command College 22

PLA Military Strategy viii

PLAN strategic submarine fleet 34

Portable Laser Distributer xvii, 42

Precision Guided Munition xvii, 26, 41, 42

Pre-emptive Strike 22, 28, 30, 58

Program 863 23, 60, 61

R

Rapid Reaction Forces xvii, 19

Revolution in Military Affairs x, xvii, 18, 40, 59

Rocket Propelled Grenade xvii

S

Sea Lines of Communication xvii, 10, 13, 33

Second Artillery 34, 35, 36, 75, 80

Senkaku Islands 7, 8, 28

Shashoujian v, vii, xi, xv, xvi, xvii,

INDEX

14, 20, 21, 22, 23, 24, 25, 26, 27, 28, 29, 30, 31, 32, 33, 34, 37, 40, 41, 43, 44, 47, 48, 50, 51, 61, 64, 80, 82. *See also* Assassin's Mace

jian meaning sword or mace 20

sha meaning kill 20

shou meaning hand 20

Shashoujian in War Fighting Strategies

  employing the Assassin's Mace in a time phased manner 25

    actual conduct of war 26

    Pre-emptive strikes 26

    Strategies prior to declaration of hostilities 26

  War Fighting Strategies v, xi, 25

Shashoujian Weapons

  Air Based xv

  Air Based Shashoujian (ABS) 23, 41

  Land Based xvi

  Land Based Shashoujian (LBS) 23

  Oceanic Strike xvii

  Oceanic Strike Shashoujian (OSS) 23

  Space Based xvii

  Space Based Shashoujian (SBS) 23, 41

Ship Submersible Ballistic missile Nuclear xvii, 32, 92, 96

Shkval rocket torpedo 64

Short-Range Ballistic Missile xvii, 80, 81

Sittwe 11

Sovremenny Class 35

Space Based Shashoujian (SBS) xvii, 23, 41, 44, 45, 47, 51, 59

Space Warfare 53

Special Operation Forces xvii

Spratly Island 28

Straits of Malacca 9, 76. *See also* Malacca

Stratagems 36 3

Subic Bay 12

Sunda Strait 76

Sun Tzu 2, 3, 40

Surface-to-Air Missile xvii, 63

Surface to Surface Missile xviii

T

Taiwan x, 7, 8, 9, 13, 14, 16, 35, 47

Terminal High Altitude Defence xviii

Theatre Information Systems 32

Thermobaric Weapons 55, 56

Three Warfares concept 19

  Legal Warfare 19

  Media Warfare 19

  Psychological Warfare 19, 29

Tibetan Autonomous Region xviii, 6

U

Ultra High frequency xviii

Unmanned Aerial Vehicle xviii, 29, 49, 67, 78, 86

Unmanned Combat Aerial Vehicle xviii, 34, 49

Unmanned Combat Platforms xviii, 26, 28, 30, 32, 37, 48, 77

Unmanned Underwater Combat Vehicles xviii, 50

Unmanned Underwater Vehicles xviii, 49, 50

X

Xi Jinping 8

Xinjiang x, 11

W

War Fighting Strategies v, xi, 25

www.ingramcontent.com/pod-product-compliance
Lightning Source LLC
Chambersburg PA
CBHW030222170426
43194CB00007BA/830